THE
PLAIN MAN'S GUIDE
TO SECOND-HAND
FURNITURE

The
Plain Man's Guide
To Second-Hand
Furniture

FRANK DAVIS

LONDON

MICHAEL JOSEPH

First published in Great Britain by
MICHAEL JOSEPH LTD
52 *Bedford Square*
*London, W.C.*1
AUGUST 1961
SECOND IMPRESSION JANUARY 1962
NEW EDITION NOVEMBER 1971

© 1961 *by Frank Davis*

7181 0936 8

*Printed lithographically in Great Britain by
Hollen Street Press Ltd at Slough and bound
by James Burn at Esher, Surrey*

CONTENTS

ILLUSTRATIONS

Photographs

vii

Drawings in text

ACKNOWLEDGEMENTS

My grateful thanks to the following for permission to illustrate:

The Victoria and Albert Museum, the seven original drawings and plates 18, 19; The Council of Industrial Design, plates 14, 17, 27, 29, 30; Messrs. Barnard's, Norwich, plates 23, 24; Dr G. Hughes, plate 28; H. Myer & Co. plate 25; Alexandre Georges, N.Y., plates 12, 13; The President and Fellows, Queen's College, Cambridge, plate 6; Mrs. H. Smorthwaite, plates 10, 11, 22; Christie's, plate 13; Sotheby's, plates 2, 4; Knight, Frank & Rutley, plate 9.

I am greatly indebted to Mrs Betty Bradford for the care she took over the drawings.

Finally, warm thanks to N.G.D. for constructive, down-to-earth, good-humoured criticism.

Foreword to the 2nd Edition
1971

I was surprised – and of course pleased – to learn that this little book of ten years ago was still enjoying a modest popularity; I was still more surprised and pleased, on rereading it, to discover that I did not want to alter a word in spite of the general increase in prices of reasonably good furniture since 1961, the lively interest in anything that can be described as Art Nouveau (from a lamp by the great Tiffany of New York to a delicate glass by the even greater Emile Gallé of Paris) the popularity of antique fairs up and down the country, and the interesting phenomenon, in London at least, of Antique Markets – extensions in more comfortable surroundings of the Caledonian Market of yesteryear. But all these activities, though not without relevance, are not the subject of this book, which pursues the humbly possible rather than the rare and unlikely, and at the same time endeavours to show certain standards of design which, on the whole, have provided the basis upon which later generations have built.

One will have no difficulty, for instance, in deciding that the simple pattern of the chair No. 15 in the illustrations is a modified version of one of the elegant Sheraton designs reproduced facing page 31. In the same manner the modern steel chair of No. 13 is a legitimate descendant of its neighbour, the elegant bent-wood chair by Thonet of the 1830s. I venture to emphasize such points because people are tempted to believe that new materials and new methods of using old materials necessarily mean a break with tradition; what one generally finds, on looking a little further into the past, is that entirely fresh design ideas are of the rarest occurrence and that the clumsiest of, say, Victorian what-nots, apparently put together by a demented wedding-cake manufacturer, has quite a respectable ancestry, going right back to the 16th century oak court cupboard, which, originally, was literally a cup board, upon which a householder of any consequence would display his silver. Follow this solid, practical design down through the centuries, you find yourself looking at an infinite variety of, on the one hand familiar dining room sideboards and, on the other, some quite simple two- or three-tiered, light sidetables (the French étagères), – page 50 – later developing into today's ingenious collapsible wheeled trolleys which are so often the answer to a maiden's prayer in the normal cramped quarters of today.

We are, though, still left with the problem of what exactly do we mean by second-hand as opposed to other furniture. It is obviously not just furniture which happens to have changed owners, for that definition would apply to all the finest pieces in the world, many of which have found new homes not once or twice but ten or twenty times. I would rather say that 'second-hand', as it is discussed here, is furniture which has fallen out of fashion and which may – or may not – someday rise in the social scale. It can also include all kinds of apparently original pieces which may have cut a dash in some very grand auction rooms and galleries in the past and which, since their days of glory, have been discovered to have been composed of several unrelated bits – the result is not necessarily displeasing but is too obviously the progeny of an unholy union without benefit of clergy or even of a registrar.

There is also that vast array of furniture, some of it very solidly and honestly made, which has been turned out not by the thousand, but by the million during the past hundred years or so. These pieces are not so distinctive as the drawing of the Windsor armchair (Fig. 2, page 15) which happens to be a pattern derived from the past by Jack Goodchild (d. 1950) who was among the last of the sturdy individual chair-makers of the High Wycombe neighbourhood – but the innumerable chairs of this type originally for farm and kitchen use which, mostly of beech with seats of elm, were built to stand up to rough treatment and have triumphally survived. They and their variants are among the most sensible things produced for the mass market during the past fifty years and no modest household need be ashamed of them.

The fact is that the Plain Man, uninhibited by the snobbery of fashion and poking around amid the deliberate squalor of the average junk shop can still, if fairly strong-minded and reasonably lucky, find presentable odds and ends which are not uncomely for a pound or two which he may decide are much easier to live with than many an expensive object 'a la mode.

The 1961 edition of this little book was criticised for daring to include in the category of 'second-hand', chairs and trays made of papier-mâché. I agree that was – and still is – heresy, for many persons dote on the stuff and well made and unusual pieces, particularly if composed wholly of the material and not just a wooden base covered with it, fetch uncommonly high prices. But while an occasional piece from the early period of papier-mâché is bearable – the originator of the material, (paper pressed together, oiled, varnished and baked) Henry Clay of Birmingham, initiated the process in 1772 – most of what survives dates from about 1840 to 1875 and so appeals chiefly to those tough enough to be able to live with the more extravagant sort of Victoriana. The stuff is, in short, as modish and as admired as is waxed fruit beneath a glass case – and so I remain unrepentant at having included it in this unmannerly survey.

The other pursuit of course which can sometimes be rewarding for the open minded uninhibited poker around is of course still the off-beat auction-room, by which I do not refer to the trick auction gentlemen who used to operate in temporarily leased premises in the Strand, but highly proper and respectable firms who conduct minor dispersals in suburbs and country far removed from the rarefied atmosphere of Bond Street or King Street, St. James's, and in so doing perform a most important economic function – that of distributing ordinary household goods from where they are not wanted to where they are. I admit that search for what one wants by this method takes time but if one has leisure it can be vastly entertaining as well as rewarding. It is all such a lucky – or unlucky – dip, and, even if one meets with disappointment after disappointment, there is always the consolation of reading the catalogue. He is surely a dull dog, a Plain Man beyond the ordinary standards of plainness, who fails to have his imagination sirred by such items as this,

A dwarf mahogany cupboard with 2 panel doors, 26in., a 2-tier book table, an oak table on spiral legs, 31in., 2 wicker elbow chairs, a walnut cane-panelled linen box with sliding top, 20in., and 2 Windsor chairs

A walnut square-top 2-tier occasional table, a mahogany open bookcase, a directory holder, an enamel-top kitchen table, 2 green painted chairs, a ditto stool, a bathroom cabinet, a linen basket, a wine rack, a sack trolley, a pair of steps, a folding luggage stand, a standard lamp, an ironing board, 2 sleeve boards, a 4-fold screen, 2 baskets, and a towel airer

A page or two further on, one comes across these, no less intriguing,

A Regency style inlaid mahogany circular 2-tier revolving bookcase with brass gallery top on column and tripod supports, brass paw feet 18in.

A Victorian burr-walnut kidney-shaped pedestal writing table with 9 drawers, slides at sides, inset top and baize-lined protector, 45in.

An antique oak coffer with a rising top, carved and panelled front, 40in.

A 5ft. mahogany sideboard with 2 panel doors, 2 centre drawers, having blind feet ornament, on square legs.

A walnut and banded bow-fronted bedroom suite of a 2-door wardrobe on cabriole legs, 36in., a knee-hole dressing table with 5 drawers, plate glass top, 42in., a chest of 2 short and 3 long drawers, 30in., a bedside cupboard, and a 4ft. panel-end bed with spring and mattress.

Finally – (one must stop somewhere) – if your tastes run to the slightly exotic and you have a pound or two to spare – there is this:

Two African drums, a hide shield, 10 spears, 3 swords, a bow and sheaf of arrows, 3 clubs, 2 sticks, and 2 3-prong spear heads.

With luck you may have acquired all this for about £50. Some of it may be too horrible to live with, but at least if you are young and hard up it will provide nearly half a houseful much of which you will joyfully discard as you grow more prosperous, while the better pieces, after a year or two of care and attention, will very likely have become such familiar household goods that you will never have the heart to see them go. Still more intriguing is the possibility that one piece out of all this may, in due time, turn out to be something that all the best people have been looking for for half a century – an original design by some nearly forgotten man who has been dug out of obscurity and recognised as well above the average. Remember though the principle of *caveat emptor* – let the buyer beware, for auctioneers make no guarantee. This is particularly necessary in the case of carpets and rugs; if you pay more than you can afford for a Persian rug and discover later that a corner is moth eaten and that it was originally two feet longer, a slice having been cut out and the two remaining sections neatly sewn together, do not blame anyone but yourself. You have eyes in your head and though, strictly speaking, the cataloguer could have pointed this out, he may be dealing with one hundred rugs in a single morning and is only human. What is more you will very possibly have acquired it for a fiver, whereas had it been in better condition you would have had to pay anything between £50 and £100.

I should say that during the past ten years most people have become a good deal more knowledgeable about furniture and are not quite so likely to confuse geese with swans as they were when this book was first published. More especially I think they have become more familiar with the styles in favour at any particular period and have learnt to look at most pieces with a more critical eye. That means they more readily distinguish between what has been made up from various odds and ends (which I would classify as second-hand) and a sound original piece which may have suffered a good deal from the normal family hazards but requires only very minor repairs. I must repeat – 'second-hand' – in the context in which it is used here is a very wide term which every man will no doubt interpret in his own fashion. To many it will seem to imply just grubby, unlovely junk with no pride of ancestry. But that is too narrow a definition. I suggest rather that it refers to a whole battery of serviceable objects which, though far from the standards of Chippendale and Hepplewhite, are by no means rubbish and with which the impecunious, by taking thought, can avoid the appalling prices of so much mass-produced, ill-made furniture of today.

I must say a brief word about prices. It is true that since the first edition of this little book was published ten years ago the prices of the rare and finer kinds of furniture have risen alarmingly. But exceptional pieces are not our concern; it still remains a fact that of the many thousands of objects which pass through the opulent portals of Christie's and Sotheby's about two-thirds find new homes at less than £100, while the pattern of the ordinary, down-to-earth furniture sale remains very much as it was set out on pages one and two of that edition. I took as a sample an actual furniture sale of two hundred lots – goodish, poor and very, very ordinary – which realised £7,000, that is an average of £35 each; but £1,500 of this total was provided by five pieces only. We hear a great deal about record sums paid for the exceptional; the normal humdrum work-a-day dispersal is not news. The magic resides in thousands of pounds and in famous names. To sum up – given patience and of course time and a share of good luck it is still possible to acquire furniture which is not too nasty to live with at anything between £5 and £50. At that sort of price one must not of course be too choosy, but there is still decent, unpretentious stuff about within most people's reach. I am writing for the impecunious. Let them take heart, cultivate a sceptical eye, avoid shoddy three-piece suites and similar horrors and shop around cocking a snook at fashion.

Chapter 1

As far as Fleet Street is concerned, when it condescends to take a brief look at the auction rooms and the dealers, big money is news and little money is not. As the great majority of us are little-money men and women who cannot possibly afford to pay £200 for a single 18th-century chair, still less £1,900 for a set of six (as happened the day before I started to write this book) or 5,500 guineas for a set of eight (as happened a week later) it is reasonably safe to say – as Fleet Street presumably knows its business – we enjoy reading about these and similar extravagances without having very much hope of indulging in them ourselves. What we are, I think, liable to miss because of this newspaper obsession with high prices, is that while all these and many other sensational sales are continually occurring, they are the high spots and not the normal. I am looking through a catalogue of a furniture sale at this moment. There were 200 lots, and the total obtained for them was £7,000 – an average of £35 each lot. But £1,500 in this quite ordinary kind of sale was provided by five pieces only – exceptional pieces without being wholly out of this world. That means that 195 lots were sold for £5,500 – and that works out at about £21 per lot. That also means that some went through for £5 and a few for maybe £50. In other words, the notion put into our heads by all the ballyhoo about priceless treasures and so forth is very largely ballyhoo and no more. It also means that the searcher for the pleasant and unusual piece with some pretensions to character, decent workmanship and even charm need never be afraid to look around the grandest and most famous of auction rooms; given patience and a refusal to be stampeded he is likely to find something within his means nearly every time. None the less, many of the objects discussed in the following pages will not be found – not yet anyway – in the most dignified, not to say august surroundings. For some it will probably be necessary to go out into the highways and hedges; in either case, good fun and good hunting is to behad, and there is ample opportunity of listening to a great deal of good sense and sometimes delightful and impudent nonsense: as when, way down in Devonshire, a nice man proved to me that the very feeble watercolour he owned was unquestionably by Whistler. 'See that man looking over the bridge at the river,' he said. 'See the big hat he's wearing! Well, Whistler always wore a big hat – so he's put himself in, see – put himself in his own picture – better than a signature, isn't it?'

It is a common heresy – and again I'm afraid Fleet Street is partly responsible – that anything old is valuable and that anything which we label second-hand is not – *ipso facto* not. Of course, everything which we don't buy directly from a shop or the maker is technically second-hand, from the finest Chippendale set of ladder-back chairs down to the brass bedstead we paid the dustman to take away and which he unloaded on to the junk shop round the corner for 2s. 6d. And here we become involved in all kinds of subtle distinctions of judgment and taste and prejudice, for each generation – each decade for that matter – has its own notions of what is fit to live with, the bright young newly-weds of the 1760's bundling all grandmamma's Queen Anne walnut into attic or stable, and those of the 1860's treating Hepplewhite's elegant mahogany with equal contempt. I well remember, in the 1920's, going to a shop in that fascinating area in the neighbourhood of the Middlesex Hospital and seeing four rooms stuffed with very nice pieces of Dutch 18th-century walnut. Said I, 'I had no idea that there was such a demand for Dutch furniture in this country.' 'There isn't,' said the proprietor.' 'Well, then, how do you make a living?' 'This, sir,' said he, 'is Queen Anne.' 'But...' I began. He continued, 'It's like this. I know and you know that all this stuff here is Dutch and I import it from Holland. Very well, I call it Dutch and I live with it for the rest of my life; but I call it Queen Anne, and I have to buy a fresh consignment every three months.' It was as simple as that at that particular time – and then fashion changed, people became more knowledgeable and Dutch furniture of good quality is both recognised and cherished for what it is and is welcomed back in Holland.

But to return to the popular heresy that there is

3

some special merit and therefore some special value about a thing just because it is old. What a barbarous notion! – as if nobody did rubbishy or clumsy work until our own day? As if clots and bunglers came into the world only at the accession of Queen Victoria! The truth surely is that most of what has survived was made by good craftsmen for the more comfortably situated members of society; less fortunate people, in a simple economy, made shift with the fairly rough work of the local joiner and carpenter and their productions were replaced, as prosperity spread downwards, by mass-produced furniture – a process which was beginning before Trafalgar. We are liable to flatter the distant past more than it deserves because so much of its rubbish has not withstood the assaults of time. We are liable to despise the furniture of yesterday and today because it is so difficult to steer a course through its largely uncharted shoals.

Most of us have to be content to live within our incomes and to eat on, sit on, laze on and live with pieces of furniture which are practical and comfortable rather than rare or specially distinguished. I am suggesting that there's no shame in having to make do with the second – or even the tenth – best when needs must, but in order to recognise the second-best when you see it it is necessary to have some small acquaintance with the higher flights of cabinet-making. Herewith, in Plates 1 to 6 between pages 24 and 25, six notable pieces of 18th-century furniture – French and English – for use as a yardstick, in the certain knowledge that only by a million-to-one-chance will any one of them fall to your predatory eye for a few pounds. But whereas the cabinet-maker, working in London for the best people, produced during this century some superlatively fine furniture, almost as a matter of course, these famous patterns were simplified and imitated in an infinite variety of ways outside the magic limits of St Martin's Lane, where Thomas Chippendale had his workshop. The difficulty begins just at this point: to distinguish between the good and the ordinary. My experience is that those who happen to own a goose are not often too pleased to be told that the creature is not in fact a swan; the way to make sure is to study swans so that unless you are specially obtuse you can recognise them when you see them without lengthy demonstrations.

But these six pieces are indubitably swans.

Plate 1 is a delicately balanced toilet table in kingwood and inlaid with various woods – where visible in this illustration, river landscapes and buildings within rosewood borders. The top is inset with a leather panel. The interior is no less exquisite – adjustable toilet mirror, two divisions with lifting corners, and the panels of these covers inlaid with a musical trophy and bouquet of flowers. The top has an ormolu border and ormolu scroll and foliage toes. In short, a gem of mid 18th-century Paris cabinet-making.

Plate 3 is staunchly English, sedate and in its way no less distinguished. Date, about 1710, material walnut, carving on the knees, scroll and feet and a curve in the upper drawer. A writing bureau, and the great-great-great-grandmother of many thousands of offspring down to our own day (compare with

Plate 20) – the majority of them recognisably of the family but without the quiet good manners of their ancestress. The fall-down front will rest on the two slides, the ends of which are seen beside the upper drawer, and inside is the usual arrangement of small drawers and pigeon holes. The type began as a movable writing box on a table, then grew into this single piece, frequently with drawers down to the ground and sometimes with shelves for books above almost reaching to the ceiling.

Plate 2 is also a distinguished English ancestor; a card table of about 1780 or so, of beautifully figured and beautifully carved mahogany; the carving crisp and precise, the proportions nicely adjusted, top and sides gently curving. The top opens out, of course, and the general proportions, with straight legs and straight sides, or semicircular sides, without carving, with slight permutations and combinations, sometimes of high, often very low, quality workmanship, have been the stock-in-trade of every furniture store ever since.

Plate 4 is a giltwood armchair of the late 18th century, English but in the French manner of the day, and covered with Beauvais tapestry – a type which has been the model for innumerable salon chairs of the 19th century. Examples, of a certain poor-relation quality, are to be found in quantity.

Plate 5 is a fine mahogany chair of about 1785, a workaday Hepplewhite type with crisp carving of hanging silk and wheatears. The simple chair of Plate 15 is illustrated as one of an immense variety of patterns of, I suggest, the 1880's which ultimately

6

derive from this; no carving, no shaped cresting, but still well-mannered and solidly made – and well worth the £3 it cost during the war.

Plate 6, early 16th century, is a famous turned chair preserved at Queen's College, Cambridge, and mentioned briefly in the following chapter.

I repeat: if these and other swans are studied with care, we can proceed without illusions to search for the more or less agreeable geese which follow.

For the best part of a century now the words Chippendale, Adam, Hepplewhite and Sheraton have ORIGINAL DESIGNS passed into the language as descriptive of particular 18th-century styles. A few illustrations from their designs may help the reader to find his way about amid the confusing jumble of objects which have been made since their day. Most people are of the opinion that nothing specially original has been evolved since, unless we include the latest chairs and settees with spindly metal legs and extremely clever comfortable springing. In general, most of the furniture one is likely to find in out-of-the-way corners will be derived in one way or another from these designs; sometimes honest, well-made copies or sensible adaptations, like the balloon chairs of the 1850's and 60's. Nearly forty individuals in the 18th and early 19th centuries, great and small, obscure and famous, have left behind them some record of their designs for furniture, either as drawings or as published books, but these four are by far the best known.

Robert Adam (1728–1792), of course, had many other interests besides designing furniture; he was architect, builder and arbiter of taste in addition, for in designing you a fine house, he would design everything in it from attic to fire-irons. Of the other three – two were practical cabinet-makers running their own business. *Thomas Chippendale* (*c.* 1718–1779) came to London from Yorkshire in 1748 and became famous from his publication *The Gentleman and Cabinet-Maker's Director* 1754 – a fine folio which has resulted in his achieving a reputation which is possibly excessive. Other craftsmen of the day who did not advertise in this highly successful and dignified manner were no less competent. *George Hepplewhite* (d. 1786) is a very shadowy figure and the book which bears his name, *The Cabinet-Maker and Upholsterer's Guide*, was not published until two years after his death. No bills for his furniture are known and very little furniture corresponds exactly with his plates in the book. None the less, his name is a convenient label – understood by everyone – to describe a chair with, say, a heart-shaped pierced back or with Prince of Wales feathers.

Thomas Sheraton (1751–1806) was a journeyman cabinet-maker for many years until he turned author and, in addition, became a drawing-master. His first book of designs was published in 1793–4: *The Cabinet-Maker and Upholsterer's Drawing-Book*, in which he criticises the Hepplewhite book as old-fashioned. Before his death in 1806 he, and others, had realised that there was much to be said for chair legs which were sabre shaped – a characteristic of a great deal of furniture of the first twenty years of the 19th century.

Between pages 40 and 41 are seven engravings or drawings of chairs – original designs of the 18th century. Not all of them were actually manufactured exactly as published, but a close study of them shows very clearly what their designers had in mind.

A. In the middle years of the 18th century bogus Chinese designs were very much *à la mode*. Here are three of Chippendale's very fanciful notions of what Chinese chairs might be. He suggests in each case how a plain leg and stretcher can be elaborated. They appear in the first edition of *The Director* (1754) but are dropped from the third, of 1762.

B. Chippendale again showing three versions of the famous riband-back design; more difficult and not nearly so practical as the more familiar ladder-back. He wrote: 'If I may speak without vanity, the best I have ever seen (or perhaps have ever been made).'

C. A drawing by (or to the ideas of Chippendale) for an armchair of about 1760. Simplify this, coarsen it and substitute heavy, clumsy turned legs for the carved cabriole legs of the drawing and you can see what commercial firms in the 1860's made of this basic idea.

D. A drawing of six chair backs by Chippendale made for the 1762 edition of the *Director*. Far more practical than the riband-back design of *B* but still requiring highly-skilled workmanship.

E. A drawing by Robert Adam. A design for an armchair for Osterley Park, 1777. Six of them are still in the state bedroom at Osterley. A very special order, of course, but a good example of the great man's

9

brilliance in seizing upon both French and classical designs and making them into something of his own. An ancestor of thousands of simpler drawing-room chairs.

F. More ancestors, this time from the Hepplewhite book published in 1788. All the plates are dated 1787. Hepplewhite calls this kind of chair 'banister-back chair,' a name which has long gone out of use. He says they are usually made of mahogany 'with seats horse-hair, plain, striped, chequered, etc., at pleasure.'

G. Sheraton makes a point here of rectangular-type backs, but still in No. 5 retains the Hepplewhite heart shape.

Chapter 2

This book then is largely concerned with inverted CHAIRS
snobbery, substituting a perverse passion for the
unfashionable for a modish liking for whatever is
temporarily favoured by the best people. Some day
perhaps it will even be quoted by solemn students of
sociology as evidence of the tendency of the despised
oddments of one generation to become the admired
decorations of the next. Certainly a good many junk-
shop bits of rubbish of yesterday are the darlings of
auctioneers and dealers of today, so that I can scarcely
wait for this book to be written and printed lest the
market for one or two of the things I propose to talk
about rockets upwards in the meantime. Too bad if I
recorded a find of a dignified – no, a distinguished –
brass bedstead for £1 and then discovered by the
time that appeared in print, not even an undis-
tinguished, battered brass bedstead was obtainable
anywhere under £50. This sounds mere foolishness,
yet it is the sort of thing which has happened in the
past and which I can perhaps illustrate by a reminder
of what has happened to the homely Windsor chair
within the memory of many of us. This will also

perhaps help to define more closely what is meant by the term 'second-hand,' which we use loosely enough and very frequently to denote something definitely scruffy.

'Antique,' on the other hand, has come to imply a certain cosy romanticism and by now is a word of the highest respectability so that when – as I read recently in a newspaper – an American gentleman protested that it was obvious that he was highly thought of, for was he not a director of the largest company of manufacturers of antique furniture in the country, nobody laughed. Windsors have been manufactured in various parts of these islands, but mainly in the beech woods round High Wycombe, since the early years of the 18th century. How they acquired their name no one knows, though one can be reasonably sure that the story current for the past half-century at least that George III, dropping in one day at a humble house in the neighbourhood, expressed his approval of their simplicity, is merely agreeable sales talk. With their stick backs of various shapes and mostly elm seats they were practical, cheap, and perfect examples of a rustic industry. The type was adapted also for the wide open spaces, and the American colonies produced distinctive and very pleasant variations upon the same theme. They were most decidedly not made for great houses though they were well enough for the kitchen staff; their main markets were the farming community, pubs, the vast and growing middle class and in due course the labourer. For at least a century and a half they were despised as useful but vulgar and then nostalgic lookers-backward, egged on enthusiastically by the dealers, discovered virtues in them which had hitherto passed unnoticed. The whole subject of Windsors has been investigated, pontificated upon, rhapsodised over, analysed, explained and illustrated with the result that no one is any longer ashamed to be the owner of a quite ordinary Windsor chair, and the price of the unusual has soared beyond the ambitions of most of those who manage to read this book. I take it that neither the Plain Man nor his Handsome Wife proposes to pay as much as £100 for a single chair. None the less, if one does not set one's sights too high there are good honest Windsors of about the 1850's or later to be found for a song (or one or two songs) which are fit to live with and can – at the moment at least – come under the category of second-hand – or, maybe by now, twentieth-hand. What it actually boils down to is that though anything which is not in the possession of its original owner is technically second-hand, ordinary usage confines the term to pieces of no great consequence, things which are not museum or collectors' items *as yet*. Half a century ago all Windsors would no doubt have come within the scope of this book. Now that the rarer types have risen so much in the social and financial scale, one will be lucky indeed to find any but the simpler Victorian – or at most early 19th-century – ones in the little shop round the corner.

Perhaps two sorts of Windsors will be of interest at this point – the one very nearly unobtainable, the other of a sort which has been made from the beginning of the 19th century down to our own day. Fig. 1

fig. 1

is a drawing of the chair in the Victoria and Albert Museum known as the Goldsmith chair. This is one of the few surviving chairs of any kind – Archbishop Juxon's is another – which have authentic associations with a well-known person. It was bequeathed by Oliver Goldsmith, on his death in 1774, to his friend Dr William Hawes, founder of the Royal Humane Society, and remained in the doctor's family until it was given to the Museum in 1872 by the widow of Sir Benjamin Hawes. One can be quite sure that this is a type which was made about the middle of the 18th century, and he will be a bold man indeed who will be prepared to argue that it was not repeated during many subsequent years. I repeat that it is most unlikely that its twin will turn up unrecognised in a country dealer's shop. Such a thing as Fig. 2, well made and anything from about a hundred to ten years old, can scarcely be classed as uncommon and comes well within the second-hand furniture class; not yet recognised as worthy of intensive search, but as honest and as practical and as comely a type of Windsor as anyone could wish – a pattern made by the dozen by a first-class chair-maker of Naphill, near High Wycombe – Jack Goodchild, who died as recently as 1950. The centre splat – the wheel back – is a feature of Windsors since the beginning of the 19th century at least. Do not, by the way, despise a Windsor chair which is painted black or green. Most

14

so that the sometimes but not invariably well-bred
geese which follow are easily recognisable. Supporting the seven original designs from
the 18th century.

1. Mid 18th-century
Paris toilet table

2. Late 18th-century
mahogany card table

3. Early 18th-century walnut bureau

4. Late 18th-century gilt armchair

5. Mahogany chair of the 1780's

6. 16th-century 'Erasmus Chair'

of us prefer them in their natural wood, polished by use, by wax and by elbow grease – but they were frequently sold painted.

fig. 2

Of all the minor household goods which have survived the passage of the years, chairs must be the most numerous in spite of a staggering amount of casualties. It has to be a fairly tough wooden contraption to stand up to the tiltings, horse-play, kicks and rumbustiousness of several generations of children; this is no doubt the reason why so many rather fine, grand chairs have survived while their humbler contemporaries have disappeared. The former were kept largely for ceremonial occasions in great houses while the latter had to submit to rough treatment. One is therefore liable to credit our predecessors with somewhat higher standards than they actually achieved. That these standards were very high indeed for pieces destined for the best people scarcely requires demonstration. The gradual emergence of a middle class with a liking for comfort, an eye for style and a not wholly unworthy desire to have around them furniture comparable with that of their social superiors, was sufficient to encourage cabinet-makers to modify their more elaborate patterns to meet this new market. But all this came about in a sophisticated age. The earliest domestic chairs which have survived – obviously The Coronation Chair is far too grand a chair of ceremony to be discussed here – are simple constructions by either the turner or the joiner. Perhaps the most famous turned chair in this country is the simple chair at Queen's College, Cambridge, associated with the name of Erasmus of Rotterdam – a wonderfully elegant shape for all its rough construction. (See Plate 6.) Early joined chairs, generally of oak, evolved reasonably enough from a stool or bench, or a box by the addition of a back and arms. The few of this sort which are in existence are frequently decorated in the back panel with a floral or chequer-board inlay, while there is generally some kind of scrolling cresting at the top and projecting ears at the sides. With all such things it is tempting to place them way back in the 16th century, or at least the first half of the 17th century, because we like to think we have tidy minds and that our ancestors wanted to make things easy for us. Nonsense, of course, if only because communications were slow and it took a long time for the fashions of the little group of people round the Court to penetrate into country districts. We can be quite certain that country carpenters were making chairs and other things in the old style and in the traditional manner long after new-fangled ideas – which in this case meant the use of walnut and marquetry and veneers – became all the rage.

It is convenient, and not far from the actual fact, to place this minor revolution in the few years after the restoration of Charles II in 1660, for it was then that these hitherto scarcely known woodworking skills gradually changed the joiner and carpenter into a new species of craftsman – a cabinet-maker, who could play all kinds of pretty tricks with his beautiful materials which themselves were destined to include in the course of time an enormous variety of woods from the ends of the earth.

Obviously the only way to lighten a heavy oak chair with a back made of solid wood is to pierce the back. This was done to advantage, apparently about the middle of the 17th century, when, in the type generally referred to as 'Yorkshire,' sturdy, hooped rails take the place of the normal panel – two kinds of them which, a century later, were to reappear as four delicately carved curving rails on that most graceful of Chippendale chairs, the so-called ladder-back.

Oak then was in the main used only in country districts from about 1660. Walnut was the chief wood used for fine furniture from then until about 1725, when mahogany began to be imported and in time ousted walnut for the finest furniture. The characteristic chair of the fashionable world during the last part of the 17th century was an elaborately carved and caned type which must have been expensive to make by the standards of the day and which has survived in some quantity for that very reason – it was not subjected to rough treatment. Towards the end of the century backs have become much higher with a lofty cresting, but none of these intricate and sometimes very handsome designs can have occupied the time of the country craftsman and therefore cannot reasonably haunt the imagination of today's bargain hunters – except for one variety, which, largely because of its size, is not very much admired. This is the day-bed, a very long couch with a sloping, carved head-rest which I have known offered for sale for about £35. The spade-back walnut chair of the turn of the century with its cabriole legs – generally thought of as the typical Queen Anne piece of furniture – is also beyond our pockets and so are all the well-balanced, crisply carved varieties of the later 18th century. But it is from about 1750 that one begins to find echoes of the great world in simpler country-made pieces, and this is no doubt due to two main causes. First, the gradual emergence of a class of middling people who demanded decent furniture more or less in the fashion of the day; who were not content with having any old thing knocked up for them by the local man. Second, the steady publication of a series of pattern books which the local man could obviously modify to a very considerable extent. There were many of these books, the most famous of them Chippendale's *Director* being the first of its kind, a handsome folio volume, designed to sell his name and goods to the nobility and gentry. Others were little more than trade pamphlets, their usefulness limited to practising workmen. But even Chippendale provides alternative patterns for chair legs – cabriole (obviously rather extravagant both in workmanship and wood) and straight, thus giving a lead to less fashionable makers to produce something less expensive. This chair, Plate 7, is a good, typical example of what, for lack of a better description, can be called unpretentious country Chippendale – by which is meant not that it was produced by the Chippendale firm in St Martin's Lane for a middle-class market, but that it conforms reasonably well to the style associated with his name. The wood is mahogany, legs and stretchers uncompromisingly severe and sensible, the upper part lacking in a certain generosity of proportion – an inch less here, another inch taken off there – which, by comparison with the real thing, makes it look decidedly mean. There is no precise delicate carving in the centre nor in the two ears of the top rail nor anywhere on the pierced centre splat. The finer type would have all this and, instead of the straight legs with stretchers, finely curved legs with carved knees (probably acanthus leaves) and claw-and-ball feet. In short, this is a decent, rather nice sort of country cousin, well-bred but a trifle clumsy, and not by any means to be despised. Its colour, when I first saw it, was that warm reddish brown which comes from about two centuries of use and wax polish. When I saw it again, it had been sent for slight repair to a local know-all and had returned brashly french-polished and looked horrible. Even these modest things deserve careful beauty treatment. Plate 8 is a photograph of a mahogany chair, also very far from the company of the elect, but very sturdy and of more generous proportions, with its straight legs grooved front and sides – a rather unusual refinement in a country piece of this character. A pierced splat of this type is familiar enough during the last years of the 18th century, but in this case does not seem to make a particularly harmonious marriage with the top rail. It could be that the original splat – perhaps of a flimsier character – was broken soon after the chair was made; I have never been able to decide the point. Nor, for that matter, is it of any world-shaking consequence; by now it is an old familiar friend and well worth the fiver it cost. Oddly, it still has its original cover, a piece of embroidery in the traditional pattern known as Florentine or Flame stitch, much in favour at the time, and so called because the zigzag lines of the design resemble tongues of flame.

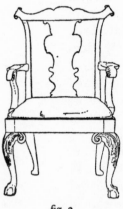

Figs. 3 and 4 are drawings of two other country-made chairs, the first possibly of the 1740's the latter of the 1790's, though no one is likely to argue the matter very closely. The point is that neither of them is very distinguished, though the maker of Fig. 3 has gone to considerable pains with the acanthus leaf carving and the ball-and-claw feet, and with the pleasant scrolling finish of the two ends of the top rail. Fig. 4 could well be from the same workshop

fig. 3

as the chair of Plate 7 but for the different pattern of the pierced slat and the grooving of the top rail. But all these are worthy representatives of many hundreds of their surviving brethren.

fig. 4

After about 1770, in the better sort of chair, legs, whether square or rounded, begin to taper towards the ground, while backs become oval, or shield-shaped, or lyre-shaped or hooped. This allowed for all kinds of variations and simplifications, with more or less near copies turned out in large quantities at intervals down to our own day; versions of some original Hepplewhite or Sheraton type, honest and quite legitimate descendants, and not made to deceive. Plate 9 is a fair sample of the better sort of chair made in quantity during the first twenty years of the 19th century. Had this book been written fifty or even twenty-five years ago, it would have qualified as a genteel second-hand chair, hopelessly out of favour with the best people. By now – and particularly since the last war – its value has soared well beyond most people's limit and it finds its place here as a well-mannered type, with numerous off-spring. The chief points about it are the scimitar-shaped front legs and the broad, slightly concave top rail. The carving on the legs and on the centre boss of the splat are agreeable refinements, as indeed are the two semicircular members of the splat; naturally, they are not to be found in less elegant pieces. These scimitar legs remained in fashion – and the slightly concave top rail – for about thirty years from 1800; it is only then that the top rail begins to be rounded and the legs become straight or cabriole once again.

Consider now the four chairs of Plates 10 and 11. They are of no great consequence and no great monetary value, but they do, I think, demonstrate the kind of good, unpretentious pieces which can be found from time to time at very small expense, given patience and a determination not to be stampeded. The chair 10a, bought at a sale in Kent, is a characteristic Hepplewhite type, with a nice elegantly-curved back and a pierced splat of the sort which, with small variations, must have been produced by the thousand during the last years of the 18th century. The straight front legs are grooved front and sides, the hooped back is moulded; there are the usual stretchers made for workaday chairs of this character – as in the chair of 8, which has a similar pierced splat not married quite so happily to the top rail. No carving of honeysuckle or husks on the back, not even paterae above the legs at each end of the seat rail; in short, hardly a chair to occupy a page of description and a photograph in a Christie or Sotheby catalogue, but a nice, honest-to-goodness middling kind of chair of its period and perhaps even providing a far more accurate notion of the furnishings of the average comfortable home of about 1790 than many of the more distinguished chairs which are very properly admired and written about as the finest things of their day. Chair 10b – the armchair – also of mahogany and also a Hepplewhite type, is a modern adaptation, but well made and I think by no means to be despised, though, when seen next to 10a, colour alone gives it away, and a certain perfunctoriness about the moulding, a lack of precision in the carving. I repeat, not a copy of an 18th-century prototype but a good commercial version of, at a guess, about the year 1900, still preserving the wide spread of the arms and a slightly curved seat rail as well as the heart-shape of a whole family of brothers sprung from the Hepplewhite pattern book.

The chair of 11a, with its grooved and turned legs and back members could well go back to about 1820. No sabre-shaped legs as in the chair of Plate 9 of about the same time – and a good deal of fiddling detail about it, especially in the centre rail of the back. Instead of the gracefully curved splat of a generation earlier leading the eye upwards to yet other curves, you have the horizontal top rail seen in the typical chair of 1810 elaborated here into this turned and reeded rail. 11b is a quite late development – my guess would be the 1880's or '90's – from both these two. All that is left of the broad top rail of the former is a little rectangular section. Arm supports and front legs are turned more or less as in 11a. To judge by the weight, this chair seems to be of stained beech. Not a masterpiece, but sensible and by no means inelegant.

The turned chair with the rush seat of Plate 14 can be regarded as a member of a most distinguished family with origins going back to medieval times. It is a descendant of such chairs as the Erasmus chair of Plate 6 and is related to the so-called Windsor with its spindle back; and, like the Windsor, was no doubt made in quantity in and near High Wycombe – and indeed up and down the country, sometimes with a spindle back as here, sometimes with a ladder back. But the Windsor proper has a hard, shaped seat of elm or ash. An armchair with a ladder back may well have five rungs and double stretchers both front and sides. This chair is obviously made for hard wear, but still has an air about it; not to be disdained, and should not be beyond a very modest purse. Compare with the William Morris version of this type in Fig. 12.

The chair of Plate 15 is a late 19th-century descendant of the fine mahogany late 18th-century chair illustrated in Plate 5. Extremely well made, solid and well mannered.

The balloon-back chair of Fig. 5a with its graceful cabriole legs, and the single carved cross-piece joining the narrow sides of the back – an important functional addition as well as a pretty one – is one of the

most charming of Victorian developments, with a fashion span of perhaps about twenty years from, roughly, the mid-1840's onwards. Details, of course, vary, also quality; the type is a reaction from the scimitar-legged chair shown in Plate 9. I have been offered eight of them for £12 each. A friend of mine bought a child's chair of this type with a cane seat with a slightly whimsical pagoda cross-piece for 7s. 6d. in Peckham High Street.

Obviously a standard shape as simple as that of the balloon back lends itself

fig. 5a

24

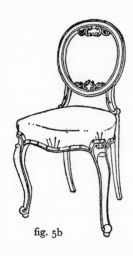

fig. 5b

to an endless variety of treatment. It can remain as plain as a bald man's head or can be subjected to any amount of elegant or inelegant carving without affecting its basic pattern. As a rule, the more carving the greater the original cost, as was natural enough. Such chairs were made by the thousand and sold in sets for bedrooms and sitting-rooms. The flimsier varieties have survived in surprising numbers. The better sort will have well-proportioned cabriole legs without stretchers, and stuffed seats, the less expensive adn the less well made cane seats and turned legs with turned stretchers. A sub-variety of the balloon back is the open oval back of Fig. 5b, a fairly simple evolution from the standard late 18th-century stuffed-back chair – merely a balloon back without a waist, with, as a rule, double scroll carving above and below – a type which remained in favour until about 1890.

The ponderous padded semi-circular-back chair of Fig. 5c, with two ugly turned legs in front and turned bars supporting the arms and back, was a popular pattern for clubs, smoking-rooms and mainly masculine

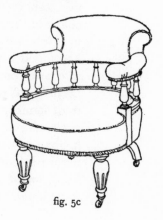

fig. 5c

gathering places from about 1870 onwards. It derives its popular name of Eaton Hall chair from a set made from Eaton Hall when that monstrous mansion was rebuilt for the Duke of Westminster in 1867.

Michael Thonet: Not at all well known, but in the long run vastly important for the chair-making industry, was an innovation by a modest cabinet-maker who lived at Bompard on the Rhine, Michael Thonet. In the 1830's he began to experiment with bending wood under heat, and was soon making chair parts, next whole chairs, from narrow, thick strips of veneer which were bent in wooden moulds and then glued together. It so happened that Prince Metternich had an estate in the neighbourhood. Before long the Prince had introduced him to the Emperor of Austria and his fortune was made; he made furniture for Prince Liechtenstein on the recommendation of an English architect, who tried, and failed, to persuade him to visit England. He was, however, an exhibitor at the Great Exhibition and is said to have sold many hundreds of thousands of his chairs in this country alone during the course of the next few years. Soon after his success with veneers he had found a means of bending solid wood and this, of course, brought further success. The majority of his products were cheap but by no means nasty. The most familiar will presumably be the simple flimsy chair with a circular seat and a back formed of two hoops, one within the other. They were made in vast numbers (not, of course, necessarily by the Thonet firm), for at least three-quarters of a century, were to be found mostly in shops and cafés, and could be piled up in pairs easily enough. Many still survive, and here in Plate 12 is one made in 1876. Next to this is a rarity – an illustration of the first bent-veneer chair made by Thonet in the 1830's. Then in Plate 13 is a type which has considerable quality – a bentwood rocking chair of about 1860, a most ingenious arrangement of curved members cunningly disposed to bear a heavy weight and at the same time with wonderfully harmonious lines. A brief article in *The Times*, March 4, 1960, on the subject of Michael Thonet and his chairs brought several letters. I quote from one of them: 'My mother belongs to the last of that generation of lovely young ladies in Vienna who swept down in their curtsies like so many white flowers to the Emperor Francis Joseph when he opened the *Ball der Stadt Wien*. She is eighty-eight years old, and told me that rocking-chairs like the one pictured were in many a drawing-room of those days. The seats of many Thonet chairs were made of complicated wicker design. In my youth I passed as soon as May had come – going to school – an old woman with a printed kerchief, sitting on a low stool on the *trottoir* of Vienna's residential district "Cottage." She repaired diligently the seat of a Thonet chair. In a basket beside her were the pieces of wicker. The old woman was Hungarian, and her work was quite expensive. But apparently she was the only one who could do the job. The Thonet showroom was very elegant in one of the corner houses of the *Ringstrasse*. The family was naturalised in Austria, and became appointed to the Imperial and Royal Court.'

Another letter recorded details of a similar chair in

the writer's possession: '. . . it differs from the one you illustrate in that the back leg has been made by bending the side scroll on itself to join the back of the chair at approximately the same position as the back leg in your illustration. Thus it has one less piece of wood on each side. Apart from the fascination evoked by its graceful lines and the ingenuity required to make the chair, the experience of rocking in it is sheer delight.' In short, a simplified version but obviously no less practical and restful. The Victorians obviously were not wholly without means of relaxing without becoming smothered in wool.

There must be many of these comely rocking-chairs in existence, though by now their cane seats and backs probably require attention. Of several proud owners known to me by correspondence, about half inherited their Thonet chairs, the remainder acquired them at sales in the country for not more than 5s. All assure me that they are the perfect garden chairs, far superior to the modern deck-chairs, though naturally they cannot be packed away into a small space. But alas – the hunt is already up! I have just been informed of one in poor condition offered to a museum for £30.

Next to it, for comparison, is a steel chair of 1926 – said to be the first chair to use the natural resilience of steel by dispensing with back legs. Designed at the Bauhaus by Mies van der Rohe. It has a leather seat and back support – and, needless to add, has had a numerous progeny both in steel and aluminium.

Chapter 3

Fig. 6 is a sociable – a true blue sociable – a mid
19th-century invention of so extraordinary a character, of such peculiar unloveliness, that it is either
hated with a fierce hatred or admired with perverse
intensity. I know one or two which are still
cherished, but I have never seen one in a second-
hand or even a whole-hearted junk shop, nor in an
auction-room; yet many were manufactured in the
1850's, and it is difficult to believe that they no
longer exist. They require a fairly large room if they
are not to become exasperating and are intended to
be placed in the middle of it. They are stuffed all
over in the most lavish manner and the two seats at
each end revolve, so that if the good ladies sitting in
them begin to quarrel they can turn their backs upon
one another and upon whoever happens to be occupy-
ing the space in between and so change the sociable
into an unsociable. Great rarities have, for obvious
reasons, been generally excluded from these pages.
The sociable has been allowed in because, odd
though it is, it is so awkward an object that if
and when it does begin to appear on the market

WOOL
STUFFING,
HORSEHAIR
AND
LEATHER

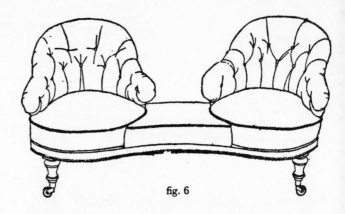

fig. 6

it is most unlikely ever to command a high price.

Plate 16 is a superbly clumsy and authentic example of the legendary horsehair sofa of about the 1860's or '70's. Short turned legs, curly half back padded head rest, leather covered. Such things certainly exist in quantity, though often with the leather worn away in patches and with the horsehair showing through – and horsehair, besides being unsightly except in its original place at either the kicking or the biting end of a horse, is extremely uncomfortable to sit on. The cushion here happens to be a well-chosen example of Berlin woolwork, and sofa and cushion formed a corner of a room of the exhibition held in London in 1951 in honour of Sherlock Holmes.

Smaller sofas of the same and similar breeds are to be found for very little, particularly if one is not scared off by dilapidated upholstery which I admit can be revolting to both sight and touch. Unless one is fortunate enough to have unearthed in the attic a fine 18th-century piece, in which case the most

a. Chippendale. 'Chinese Chairs.' Engraving 1753.

b. Chippendale. Riband Back Chairs. Engraving 1754.

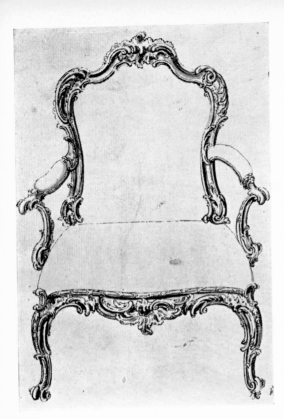

c. Chippendale. Armchair.
Drawing about 1760.

d. Chippendale. Six chair
backs. A drawing for the
1762 edition of *The Director*.

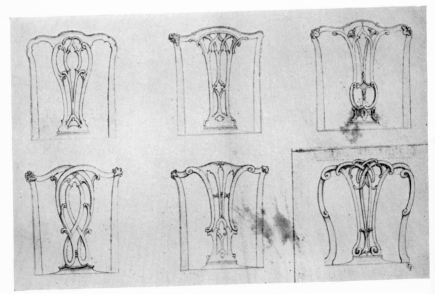

c. Robert Adam. Armchair for Osterley Park. Drawing 1777.

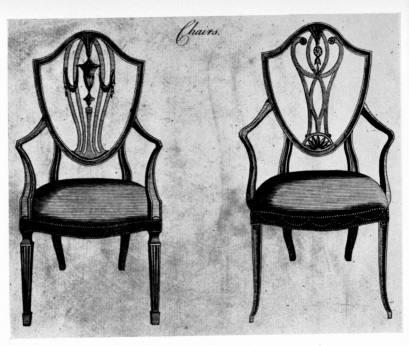

Chairs.

f. Hepplewhite. Two chairs. Engraving 1787

g. Sheraton. Six chair backs. Engraving 1792.

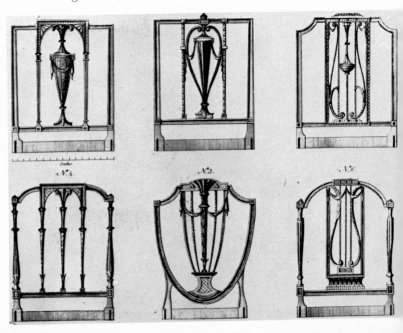

expert repair is imperative regardless of expense, the following procedure is recommended:

Rip off all the old upholstery, whether horsehair or wool, and burn it forthwith; only thus can one feel purified. If the frame is in good condition – and frames often are – do small repairs with plastic wood and clean off surface dirt. Exposed portions will frequently be of rosewood or mahogany, in which case you may well decide to keep them as they are. If not, paint them after rubbing down with glasspaper – a labour demanding a good deal of patience but well worth it. Then upholster with webbing and latex foam (two inches thickness). Cover it all with a suitable material – serge, velvet, or what not; plenty of choice as to that, and as to colour, at any good furnishing shop. First tack the covering in the required position and edge with braid. Fig. 7 is taken from a pattern book of about 1870; if one is not too ham-fisted – which almost inevitably means that the work has to be done by the feminine half of the partnership – simple treatment as indicated above can work wonders.

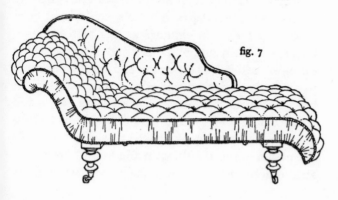

fig. 7

The chair of Plate 17 is one of those solid, clumsy, comfortable types of about 1840–1860, much in demand for clubs and smoking-rooms; well stuffed, leather covered (no such thing as synthetic leather), the short legs turned, the visible woodwork higher up carved with scrolls. It is a type which had a lengthy run and was, as far as I can see from the evidence – such as it is – made until the end of the century without much alteration. The wood chiefly rosewood, the sturdy legs ash or elm. To some a beast of a thing; to others redolent of great-grandfather's cigars. If the seat – as so often happens – is disintegrating, renewal with either leather or rexine is simple enough – but I suggest that if repairs are necessary for the back, the amateur might find the task rather formidable. By all means try latex foam and a modern material (neither leather nor a leather imitation) if you do not mind destroying the peculiar character of a chair of this kind.

PAPIER-
MÂCHÉ

Trays, chairs and various small objects made of this material, which was quite an important article of commerce in the 1840's and '50's, could have been picked up for a few shillings as late as the 1920's. Chairs especially and to a lesser degree trays became the object of a cult in the 1930's and are still admired, particularly if decked out with mother-of-pearl. A bowl of waxed fruit under a glass cover was – and perhaps still is – regarded as a desirable embellishment to a painted papiermâché tray. On the whole the material and the things made from it are rather an acquired taste, but very much the taste of today as a reaction from the angular austerities of a great deal of modern furniture.

The stuff was made by boiling up coarse paper, making a thick paste of the result and adding gum arabic. Another method: paste sheets of paper together to the required thickness; press in moulds under heat, paint with lacquer paint and polish. Chairs made from papiermâché are remarkably tough, are still to be found in odd corners and are not to be despised by any who take a nostalgic delight in the authentic atmosphere of a well-to-do middle-class early-Victorian house. Not unnaturally, far more small objects such as boxes and trays were manufactured than movable pieces of furniture which in their day would probably have been regarded as products of the novelty trade rather than as serious competitors with wood furniture. They were certainly not to be found in the average house. The chair of Plate 18 is a first-class example, from the Victoria and Albert Museum, partly painted and with flowers in natural colours, partly decorated with mother-of-pearl inlay and with cane seat. It must be regarded as about the finest thing of its kind one is likely to come across. Less dignified chairs – I am thinking at the moment of a set of six – rather narrow and with rectangular backs with a single splat, black with mother-of-pearl inlay – are, as I write, within half a mile of me, and priced at £40 the set. Very pretty little things indeed if a trifle flimsy. With ordinary luck such run-of-the-mill pieces should realise about £3 a piece in an auction; the chair of the illustration perhaps twenty times as much.

A patent for papiermâché was taken out as long ago as 1772 by Henry Clay of Birmingham; it is still used as a substitute for plaster for mouldings in interior decoration, for mirror and picture frames, etc.

BERLIN
WOOLWORK

If any one thing can be said to be characteristic of the years 1830–60 it is Berlin woolwork, so called. The term was in such common use that it was synonymous with embroidery. I quote from Mrs Henry Owen's preface to her *Illuminated Book of Needlework* (1847). 'Embroidery, or as it is more often called Berlin woolwork, has been brought to such a high state of perfection . . . the variety of patterns so great, and so well adapted to every purpose to which it can be applied . . . that we do not hope here to be able to throw much new light on the subject.' This seems a depressing conclusion which leads one to suppose that Mrs Owen was either unduly modest or naturally melancholic. In fact her performance was highly competent, as everyone sufficiently interested in the subject can see for themselves by consulting her book. They will also obtain an illuminating sidelight upon the taste of the times if they turn over the pages of Mrs Henry Wood's *A Useful and Modern Work on Cheval and Pole Screens, Ottomans, Chairs and Settees for Mounting Berlin Needlework*. This dates from about 1845 and contains eighteen plates filled with fifty designs for all kinds of furniture; Louis XIV, François I, Elizabethan, Gothic – take your choice, and all very odd. Still more odd is the fact that no attempt whatever is made to adapt the embroidery

34

designs to the various grandiose styles recommended. The craze was firmly established by the 1830's and an enormous business was done by Mr Wilks of Regent Street in both patterns and materials imported direct from Berlin. (Miss Barbara Morris, whose note on this by-way of the handicrafts in The Connoisseur Guide *The Early Victorian Period* has placed everyone in her debt, says that by 1840 no less than 14,000 different patterns had been imported into England.) No more *gros-point* or *petit-point*, the normal home embroidery for chair covers or screens, but these decidedly gross designs worked in cross-stitch or tent-stitch. Quite elaborate pictures, romantic or religious, were in favour for fire-screens and were sometimes framed and hung on the wall, but the normal chair cover was decorated with a design of monstrous blowsy flowers with sometimes a parrot or two added and in brilliant colours which have frequently faded to advantage. The backgrounds – anyway by the middle of the century – were usually black, which served to bring out the brilliance of the colours. The designs themselves were published on squared paper so that each one could be transferred easily to a square-meshed canvas; each square of the design represented one stitch. As hundreds of amateur needlewomen were busily engaged upon this very specialised kind of embroidery for at least a generation it is not surprising that quality varies considerably, nor that vast numbers of examples must exist unhonoured and either despised or unrecognised in thousands of homes.

Fig. 8 is a drawing of a typical chair of the 1850's

fig. 8

covered in Berlin woolwork – many find both chair and covering a welcome nostalgic relief from the genteel geometry of our own day. A cushion of a similar vintage is on the Victorian sofa from the Sherlock Holmes exhibition, shown in Plate 16.

BUREAUX   I suppose the most popular form of writing cabinet existing today began life in the second half of the 17th century when we were – some of us – becoming a trifle more luxurious as well as literate. A few thought it might be a sound idea to place a writing box upon a small table and keep it there permanently instead of moving the writing box about. Then came an equally bright idea – to combine writing box and chest of drawers in a single piece of furniture, with this result (Plate 3). These at first were constructed in walnut – the fashionable wood of the end of the

17th century, and were in due course made – with minor variations – in mahogany; and indeed are still made much to the same pattern in our own day. The normal arrangement is three drawers below, that is, the chest portion; an arrangement of pigeonholes and small drawers above hidden when not in use for writing by a sloping front. This falls forward to form the writing table and is supported by two wooden bars which can be pulled out when required. No one can hope to find an early original of this – or indeed of any other type – for a few pounds, but thousands of such things have been made during the past hundred years and thousands are still in service. All one has to do is to train one's eye to distinguish between shoddy and honest workmanship – a thing which can only come from experience – and reject the former, which is liable to be horridly expensive however little you pay for it.

In Plate 19 is an illustration of a particular type of writing cabinet which was a much later development and which – by some strange quirk of fashion – became popular round about the 1850's. This particular example is, in fact, an unusually elaborate and well-made piece, with its brass candlestands and beautifully chosen figured walnut. The type is called a Davenport – a name which might be thought to be a trade name chosen by chance. In fact there does appear to have been a Captain Davenport, whose name appears in the accounts of Gillows of Lancaster in the 1790's as having bought 'a desk' though there is no indication of exactly what kind of desk. Davenports are normal items in catalogues of the mid 19th century and all of them have similar characteristics: drawers at the side, turned (rarely carved) pillars supporting the projection above, frequently a brass rail at the top, and a sloping writing slab which lifts just like the desks of our schooldays. The upper portion slides forward for the convenience of the writer. I find the slope extremely inconvenient. But they are strange, nostalgic little contraptions when not too obviously shoddily made and provide a touch of cosy Victorianism. Nowadays they are becoming decidedly modish and consequently liable to be high-priced. The drawers, as in a great deal of Victorian furniture, are opened by wooden knobs, not metal. This is the case in even so comparatively luxurious a piece as the one illustrated. The use of wood for the purpose obviously cut costs, but this is a long way from the grace of the 18th century. This must not, however, be taken to mean that a 19th-century version of an earlier style will necessarily have wooden handles; far from it – metal handles were in fashion continuously, but wooden ones were used for high-class furniture to a degree which would hardly have been acceptable to an earlier generation.

The progression from the basic notion as seen in Plate 3 to dozens of other types, both old and modern, is fairly obvious – as also the development of not only adding drawers to the lower part but of bringing the whole structure nearly up to the ceiling by super-imposing a series of shelves enclosed by two doors; the doors sometimes plain, sometimes mirrors, some-times of glass; the imposing and frequently beautiful piece of furniture generally known as a bureau-bookcase or secretaire-bookcase. In this the upper part – the bookcase part – was frequently arranged so that a portion of the centre was divided in such a way that it could accommodate very tall folio manuscripts or account books. The centre portion – that is, the part revealed by the fall front – was invariably divided into an arcade of pigeonholes and beneath them a series of small drawers, with sometimes a small cupboard in the centre.

From this to the familiar pedestal writing table is but a short step. What simpler than two narrow chests of drawers with a table spread over them leaving plenty of space in the centre for one's knees? Like the little bureau of Plate 3 these also were first seen in the late 17th century and have remained in favour ever since, from carved, finely figured walnut down to fairly roughly made pieces of our own day, the former selling for many hundreds of pounds, the latter for well under fifty; these last, sometimes, with clumsy metal mounts for which more graceful substitutes should be – and can be – found without much difficulty. The point is that these types have been copied and adapted throughout the whole of the 19th century, not to mention the 20th, and are normally well within the range of modest purses. Plate 20 illustrates a fairly ordinary 19th-century version of the combined writing box and chest of drawers – mahogany and in very good condition.

Books are a problem in most houses whose inhabitants are fairly literate. It is not merely that they are liable to spread themselves around in an alarming manner, BOOKCASES

39

and indeed are almost capable of pushing their owners out altogether, but they present formidable and exasperating problems to good housekeepers. Given time and a sufficient labour force they can be kept reasonably hygienic, if not absolutely spick-and-span, when housed on open shelves. This has, of course, been the usual method from time immemorial. The glazed bookcase is a comparatively modern device, not known until the days of Samuel Pepys, whose bookcases and writing desk, now in the library of Magdalene College, Cambridge, were pioneer experiments. The 18th century saw splendid bookcases in walnut or mahogany made for country mansions, generally constructed with a carved architectural pediment of some sort or other, and frequently (particularly when the designer was Robert Adam or those influenced by him) so large as to be nearly immovable – obviously built into the room as soon as the plasterers had finished their work. I am thinking of one in a great room 30 ft by 60 ft which occupies the whole of the 30-ft wall. Bookcases of more modest proportions made up to about 1825 are to be found but at a price far beyond most pockets. What can be picked up occasionally for comparatively very little, is a Victorian version of this tradition designed for an ordinary house; something of this character (Plate 21) yet retaining the good proportions and much of the dignity of the previous century. There is nothing out of the way about the construction or design of such a piece as this. Quite nice mahogany veneers with a lighter wood for small marquetry details. The pediments are frequently missing as in this piece – to some of us no heartbreaking loss – though there are many which were made without them. The two short plus two long drawer plan is a normal arrangement and the pattern of the glazed doors is a pleasant feature. In this, as in so many other traditional types of furniture, there is a wide variety of pattern, but on the whole this photograph provides a fair sample of what one can expect to find among the humbler numbers of this large class. Drawers, in these pleasant but less distinguished bookcases, are generally nicely dovetailed in front, but rather carelessly put together at the back.

The Pembroke table is, strictly speaking, a small square table with two side flaps and was sometimes known as a breakfast table. It is supposed to have derived its name from an 18th-century Countess of Pembroke who expressed her approval of a table which could be moved easily and could be enlarged. Today, the word Pembroke is frequently used to denote what was originally, when it came into fashion at the end of the 18th century, known as a sofa table, a good modern version of which is illustrated in Plate 22b. This is a natural enough development from the original Pembroke, the flaps at each end supported upon movable brackets and with two drawers at the side. The long stretcher running the whole length is an obvious necessity. The wood was usually mahogany or rosewood or satinwood, and there were considerable variations of the underpart, the most admired of them a lyre-shaped support instead of the two simple turned pillars of the illustration. Though this table cannot be more than fifty or seventy-five years old, and though its turned members have no great distinction, it has retained certain small refinements from the past – the brass paw feet, the reeding

fig. 9

of the legs and the stringing of the drawers – which raise it much above the standard second-hand late 19th-century sofa table. As to the original small Pembroke, in the Hepplewhite pattern book they are both oval and square and they are called breakfast tables by Chippendale as early as 1754. The name was well acclimatised by the beginning of the 19th century and was used on more than one occasion by Jane Austen. (Fig. 9.). Fig. 10 shows a pedestal or card table taken from a pattern book of 1850.

DINING-
TABLES
AND SMALL
CIRCULAR
TABLES

One can easily pay two or three hundred pounds for a 16th- or 17th-century oak refectory table, sometimes, of course, a great deal more for very rare examples, or – to come closer to our own day – for one of those late 18th-century or early 19th-century

42

pedestal tables (two or sometimes three pedestals). These are – or perhaps I should say can be, for obviously not all of them are of equal quality – noble objects supported upon pedestals made of substantial turned columns each of which terminates in three curved legs and brass caps or, better still, brass paw feet. There are generally two extra leaves for extensions and, in the best examples, reeded edges;

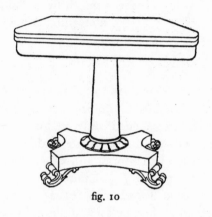

fig. 10

mahogany preferred, rosewood or satinwood by no means to be despised. As far as this book is concerned we can do no more than gaze spellbound at such dignified and elegant marvels – it would be sacrilege to cover them with even the finest damask. They are beyond our reach. Instead we have to fall back upon far clumsier confections, honest enough, but with whacking great turned legs, one at each corner; as a rule, I fear, pieces which have received a good deal of battering and upon which traces of innumerable meals have left their mark. The only drill recom-

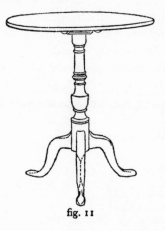

fig. 11

mended is strip and repolish.

The thing to aim at is a tripod support or supports, like that shown in Plate 22a. But modest circular mahogany tables like that in Fig. 11 can be found with luck in odd corners – or rather could once be found – for very little. Plain tripod legs, no reeding or other decoration, and very nice quality mahogany.

WILLIAM MORRIS

This is no place in which to tell the story of William Morris, of his ideals, his failures and the remarkable influence he exercised, if only indirectly, upon the decoration of the English upper middle-class house from the day when Morris and Co. was founded in 1861 with a capital of £1, an unsecured loan of £100, and premises at 8 Red Lion Square, where a small kiln was built for firing glass and tiles. The company's chief interests were wallpapers, tiles, carpets, tapestries, stained glass, and at first furniture was a secondary consideration. The earliest furniture made for William Morris was massive in form and decorated with paintings of figures or subjects from the romances of chivalry. Some of that made by the Company in its infancy was also painted, notably a Gothic canopied sideboard designed by Philip Webb, the architect, and repeated more than once. Gradually, however, cabinet work of very high quality was produced side by side with the simpler

44

carpentry productions, mostly from designs by Philip Webb and his successor George Jack. None of these are to be found in the little shop round the corner – at least I have never seen them there – but what you can find occasionally (and cheaply) are some of the firm's admirable productions deliberately made for a popular market from about 1900 onwards. That is, four years after the death of its founder. Here are a few extracts from a Morris catalogue of about 1912:

(1) Heavy oak trestle dinner table. Origin-
     ally designed by Philip Webb.
     7 ft × 3 ft 9 in £12 5 0

This is what the catalogue proudly, and I think justly, introduces in these words: 'Joiner-made furni-ture, or what may be described as Cottage Furniture, solidly made in oak, stained ash or painted pine. Specimens of this work are to be found in many of the most artistic houses in the country. They are strongly and yet neatly made, without any undue expense or superfluous finish.'

(2) Solid oak chest of drawers, 3 ft wide.
     Joiner made £8 15 0
(3) Ladder-back armchair. In green or
     brown stain ..   .. 23s. 6d.
(4) Sussex rush-seated chair. In black .. 10s. 6d.
(5) Sussex settee, 4 ft 6 in long. In black ..   35s.

The Plain Man's price indeed, and here is Pro-fessor J. W. Mackail in his *Life of William Morris* commenting upon these sensible, comely, cheap productions.

'Of all the specific minor improvements in com-mon household objects due to Morris, the rush-

fig. 12

bottomed Sussex chair perhaps takes the first place. It was not his own invention, but was copied with trifling improvements from an old chair of village manufacture picked up in Sussex (Fig. 12). With or without modification it has been taken up by all modern furniture manufacturers and is in almost universal use. But the Morris pattern of the later type (there were two) still excels all others in simplicity and elegance of proportion.'

Seats will generally require repair, but they are well worth the 10s. or £1 asked for them.

It is odd how the popular picture of this genuinely great man has become distorted. His less critical admirers paint him as a heaven-sent prophet destined to lead the people into a promised land of fine craftsmanship, good fellowship and dedicated industry, while the opposition is inclined to dismiss him as not much more than a visionary who began as a pre-Raphaelite and never grew out of the medievalism which was the besetting sin of the movement. He himself was notoriously indifferent to comfort, a fatal defect in anyone having the remotest concern with a furniture business, and his mind was far more occupied by poetry, book design, stained glass, wallpapers and paintings than by furniture. William Gaunt, in *The Pre-Raphaelite Tragedy*, refers thus to the impres-

46

7. Country Chippendale. 18th-century

8. Country Chair. 18th-century

9. Scimitar-leg chair, *c.* 1810

10a. Late 18th-century mahogany chair, Hepplewhite type.   10b. A modern variation on the same theme

11a. Chair of about 1820. 11b. A modern version of this early 19th-century type

12. Two chairs by Thonet

13. Chair by Thonet and modern steel chair

14. Early 19th-century country-made chair with rush seat

15. Late 18th-century much simplified version of Plate 5

16. Horsehair sofa. The 1850's.

17. Leather-covered chair,
1840-60

18. Painted papiermâché inlaid
with mother-o'-pearl

19. Davenport

21. 19th-century mahogany
bookcase

20. 19th century mahogany
bureau. Compare with Plate 3

22a. Walnut table about 1850

22b. Modern sofa table

No. 26.

No. 20.
Candlestick.
9¼ in. high.

No. 21.
Candlestick,
9¼ in. high.

No. 25.

Candle Bracket.

Candle Bracket with
Copper Coins.

No. 30.
A Fire Screen with bevelled edge
Glass Panel.

No. 7.

No. 8.

No. 24.
Candle Bracket, three lights.

Wrought-iron Table
with Copper Kettle
and Lamp.

Wrought-iron Table
with Copper Kettle
and Lamp.

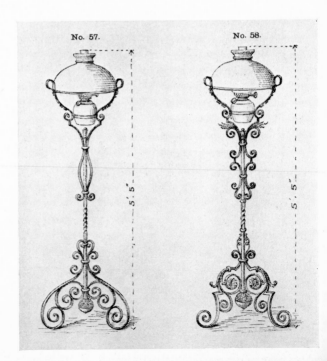

No. 57.

No. 58.

5′ 5″

5′ 5″

No. **1215**   2-in. PILLARS, ¾-in. TOP RODS, ⅝-in. PANELS 7-in. PEARL BOXES
AND PEARL SPINDLES, WITH PROJECTING PANELS.   PRICE **£18/8/6**
2/- PER SIZE DOWN.   5-FT., **10/-** EXTRA.
ALSO MADE IN FRENCH, PRICE **£15/2/6**

25. Brass bedstead *c.* 1890

26. Simple brass bedstead

27. Victorian Military Che[st]

28. We never had it so Cosy. Victorian room, late 19th-century

DINING-ROOM.

29. How to furnish a house for £250 in 1896

30. Cosy corner and other whimsies, 1896

62, 64, 67, 69, 71, 73, 75, 77 & 79, Hampstead Road; and Nos. 1 to 34, Eagle Place, London.

New design artistic Overmantel, with shaped bevelled plate, with spaces for photos, cards, &c., &c. 3 ft. 9 in. wide 72s. 6d

Hanging Bookshelf, containing cupboard with leaded glass panel 47s. 6d

New design Occasional Chair, of dark mahogany or art green stained, covered with artistic printed velvet 39s. 6d

Quaint Occasional Table, of mahogany or art green 37s. 6d

Solid mahogany Cosy Corner, with well upholstered seat and back, and covered tapestry, fitted with bookshelf, &c., &c. Suitable for library
    dining-room or hall. Can be made oak or walnut. Complete, about 4 ft. 6 in. by 3 ft. 6 in. £17   10

sions of Morris's grand-daughter, Angela Mackail: 'The impression left on her mind was one of intense discomfort. There was not a chair in the sitting-room, with its pomegranate wallpaper on a dark-blue ground, that you could sit on with ease. It was impossible to lie, or to do anything save remain rigidly erect, on the massive black sofa, whose yellow upholstery stuck to one's clothes.' Then again: 'The cushions were unyielding, the bolsters rigid.' The chairs? 'Too high in the seat, too close to the arms.' The beds? '—with their wooden slats running length-ways, banished sleep.' And this was her grandfather's own house. At the same time he could give the most admirable advice. 'That thing which I understand by real art is the expression by man of his pleasure in labour.' And again: 'Have nothing in your home that you do not know to be useful or believe to be beautiful.'

His influence? People will argue for a great many years and perhaps it is not even now possible to see him as he really was. The young man who visited the Great Exhibition of 1851 and found it wanting might have accomplished far more had he been less obsessed by the distant past, taking a medieval manuscript as a pattern for a modern book, for example. One needs more than a fervent passion for honest craftsmanship if one is to reform an industrial society, and the immediate result of his teaching was to encourage the public to demand, and the furniture manufacturers to produce, hundreds and thousands of faked antiques and reproductions; in short, the trade turned a blind eye to what he was trying to teach – a love of good workmanship – and took notice only of his interest in fashions belonging to another age.

Chapter 4

This is merely a double chest, in two sections of, THE
usually, two drawers each – and this is the point about MILITARY
it – with *sunken* brass handles on the drawers and at CHEST
the sides. It was a regulation pattern, apparently up
to about 1870, made in great quantity in mahogany
or cedar; thanks to the handles they were readily
mobile and easily packed for transport either by land
or sea. Not by any means easy to find, but well worth
pursuit as a thoroughly practical, unpretentious and
comely article of furniture – to use modern jargon, as
functional a device as ever sprang from the brain of
some unknown Q. officer (Plate 27).

Not fashionable today – indeed, out of favour since OVER-
about 1900 and dirt cheap, but not to be wholly MANTEL
despised. Usually a mirror flanked and crowned by
smallish pigeonholes for the display of china. Mahogany, pine, and frequently painted. Towards the end
of the century in genteel suburbia, bamboo.

Fashionable particularly about 1890 for overmantels, BAMBOO
small tables and cupboards. Rather finicky, not

49

inelegant, stronger than it looks and should be obtainable (when discovered) for shillings rather than pounds. Returning to favour (1961) in *dernier cri* décor.

ÉTAGÈRES This is a polite term for a highly respectable piece of furniture. The translation into basic English is 'What-not.' The French word seems to have come into use in the 18th century to describe a small, elegant side table in two or three tiers – a sophisticated and frequently exquisite version of what in the 16th century in England was known as a court cupboard, originally a board or boards on which to display cups and other plate. The Victorians

made genteel pseudo-French étagères with enthusiasm and moderate success, mainly in mahogany and rosewood in imitation of 18th-century Paris marvels. But the popular commercial translation of this very useful display piece was a structure in three tiers in rosewood or mahogany with or without a lower drawer, a fretted

fig. 13

gallery on top and the upper shelves supported on turned spindle supports. 'Whatnot' has not yet become a flattering kind of word; étagère smacks of undue gentility. Put wheels on the thing, call it a trolley, and you have something useful and well-mannered. Fig. 13 shows a simple practical design from a design book of 1867; intended to be made in oak and a

considerable distance from the normal pretentious
style of the decade.

Made throughout the 19th century for music and
today in great demand to hold magazines. The
earlier varieties, frequently beautifully made in

fig. 14

mahogany with brass inlay, are outside the scope of
these notes, but later Victorian examples are to be
found, mostly with turned bobbin bars, which are
within most people's range. I illustrate a bamboo
example which presumably dates from the 1880's
(Fig. 14).

The 18th century devised some wonderfully pretty
and on the whole simple little writing cabinets for
women; not much more than a small table with a
drawer beneath and upon it at the back a simple tier
of small drawers and one or two pigeonholes. The
style originated in Paris and was adapted by the late

18th-century London cabinet-makers with admirable good taste.

A more ponderous version also reached London by about 1870 and was carried out in satinwood and mahogany during the next twenty years. As such things nearly always have a mirror in the centre they were no doubt used as dressing tables as well.

PURDONIUM A grand name to disguise the rectangular metal-lined wooden coal-box which was a well-fancied competitor of the more familiar coal-scuttle. The top padded and a favourite seat for the young. Its inventor is said to have been one Purdo. The Latin-sounding trade name has an air of cosy erudition which is part of the Victorian myth.

WORKTABLES At first sight not obvious stable companions; in fact,
AND bred in the same stable, each with pedestal support
TEAPOYS resting upon a shaped platform with four (occasion-

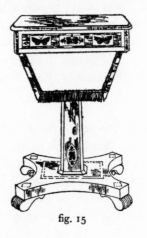

fig. 15

ally three) toes. They are clumsy but practical pieces of furniture, generally of walnut or mahogany or rosewood. The worktable would be circular or square with a hinged top revealing compartments for silks, scissors, etc. Fig. 15 shows a worktable of the 1840's decorated with Tunbridge Wells work. The teapoy opening to show velvet-lined compartments for tea of two kinds, sugar bowl, etc. Lucky the handsome wife who finds either one or the other with its accessories

fig. 16

intact; scissors are generally missing from the one, sugar bowl and caddies, whether silver or glass, from the other. Fig. 16 shows a wood and papiermâché teapoy of the late 1840's, painted in gold and colours and inlaid with mother-of-pearl.

One would imagine that in an age of compact built- WARDROBES in furniture and small flats and houses, wardrobes of some quality, though decidedly large, would be drugs on the market; that their exasperated owners would be happy to give them away. My experience has been to the contrary; I have been astonished at the prices asked in and around Tottenham Court Road for the most roughly made though pretentious Victorian wardrobes, each one of them a nightmare. My advice is, if for one reason or another built-in cupboards are out of the question, to visit the western end of the Kings Road, exercise patience and buy second-hand for a tenner one of those simple modern fitted wardrobes put out by several firms at from £20 to £30.

53

If time is available to sit out auction after auction you might acquire something neat but not gaudy of this kind for a fiver. Occasionally, though, a monstrosity can be found which is as nightmarish as any of its brethren but constructed of such splendid wood that one's heart warms to it while wondering how its designer could prostitute such finely figured materials to such a purpose. I have one such elephantine piece in mind at this moment which is doing duty as a hall cupboard. It is a tiresome, clumsy object, not nearly deep enough for its purpose, made of finely marked walnut and its door composed of a full-length mirror. Someday perhaps the mirror in its walnut frame will be taken down and hung on a wall and the remainder used to make a chest or workbox. I am not advocating wholesale destruction of furniture which happens to offend its owners' particular prejudices; it is just that some things really are beyond the pale, and not to be tolerated unless one is perverse enough to begin a collection of uglies, on the excuse that awful warnings are good for the souls of one's children and grandchildren.

There is much to be said for a wardrobe, preferably I think, of mahogany – the sort of quite simple, practical piece turned out in quantity throughout the 19th century, particularly if the interior is intelligently divided – as it frequently was – into a roomy hanging cupboard, with ample drawers on the other side; or maybe two hanging cupboards with drawers in the centre portion, and plenty of room for female hats of the largest and most glamorous description. This, I admit, demands ample space, but if that expensive commodity does happen to be available, and built-in cupboards are not possible, then a really generous old-fashioned wardrobe is not to be despised. Why live always as if one were in a small ship's cabin?

A whole series of poorly made Victorian uglies was on parade in one store at prices ranging from £70 to £100; much better sit out an auction and buy some equal horror for £20 or so. Better still, bide your time and acquire something with a little character and honest workmanship about it. For example – I have chosen at random – these two were sold in the summer of 1960 in the middle of London:

A Provençal carved walnut armoire, two doors, fitted with shelves and drawers, 4 ft 9 in wide, 8 ft 3 in high, £35.

A Flemish mahogany armoire, two panelled and shaped doors, 5 ft wide, on short cabriole legs, £30.

In a catalogue of the year 1852 which Messrs IRON AND Barnards of Norwich have been kind enough to BRASS send me, so-called Stump Bedsteads of iron, japanned dark green – that is, small bedsteads with a head rail but no foot rail – are offered at £1 1s. od. for the 6 ft × 3 ft size, £1 1s. 6d. for the 6 ft 4 in × 4 ft 6 in. Castors are 1s. 6d. extra. A half-tester bedstead with foot rail, dovetail joints, wood-bowl castors, and japanned bamboo, blue or any other plain colour costs £1 18s. od. if 6 ft × 3 ft, £2 13s. od. if 6 ft 4 in × 5 ft, with brass vases (that is knobs) 3s. extra. A folding bedstead is 16s., a child's cot with movable sides of perforated metal, 4 ft × 2 ft, £1 10s. od. Then comes the slightly sinister entry: 'Iron bedsteads for Union Houses, etc., etc. From 11s. 6d. to 14s.'

None of these, if any such survive, can be recommended, but brass bedsteads, which are by no means rare and frequently appear in country sales, when they realise, as a rule, anything from £1 to £5, are a different matter. Not that they are all things of quality, but in some cases their designers took quite uncommon pains over them. They seem to have been introduced from France as early as the 1830's. In the not over-sanitary conditions of 19th-century housing metal beds were an obvious advantage as they always have been in the tropics. For many years a combination of brass and iron was a popular commercial line in middle- and lower-class trade from the last third of the 19th century down to the end of the first world war, when – for some reason – fashion changed to wood again. A very plain 2 ft 6 in size sold for as little as 7s. 3d. in South Wales. Messrs Evereds of Smethwick tell me that one of their subsidiary firms has made metal bedsteads since 1840, and they themselves since 1884. Metal bedsteads have never lost favour in the Middle East or in Africa. The more ornamental and complicated designs appeal to persons of importance as status symbols, and there have been many instances of brass bedsteads being used as ceremonial thrones from which justice is dispensed – quite literally *lits de justice* – and even as biers at funerals. Very popular in some quarters are beds decorated in red, yellow and green on a black-enamelled background – with mirrors inset – a touch of slightly bizarre harem refinement. £400 is cheerfully paid for a bed of this type. The rather banal black metal bedstead with brass knobs is still in use in many a cheap boarding-house up and down the country and in Wales and Ireland. I illustrate a bedstead from a catalogue of about 1890 (Plate 25).

Plates 23 and 24 are from a Barnard catalogue of 1892.

Neither the table candlesticks nor the tall lamp-standards are particularly dated, could turn up in any sale or in any junk market at any moment for a few shillings, and are readily adapted for electricity. Even the candle-brackets, in spite of their rather laborious medievalism, have an air about them, and the fire screen is sensible enough. Should I ever come across either of the tables complete with copper kettle and lamp I should have to confess myself baffled; perhaps painted, and the kettle stand and lamp removed, they might still do service as a plant stand in a not too well-lighted corner. Indestructible though such things seem to be, they are today (per-haps not surprisingly) uncommonly rare.

Iron Victorian garden seats, painted white, as seen outside a little Mews house, add a touch of most agreeable nostalgia. These and other garden furni-ture can be found in some second-hand shops which make a speciality of them – and, of course, at scattered sales.

These creep into this book by a side door. They are CARPETS
mentioned because the price of new carpets of any quality is fantastic and cheap ones are not worth having. What can still be obtained by those who

have sufficient patience is a Persian rug of no great
age and only slightly worn, size from about 6 ft × 4 ft
up to 14 ft × 10 ft, for between £10 and £30. It
means spending some time in the better sort of
auction room and knowing exactly what you want.
Such floor coverings, whether placed upon boards or
upon a plain ordinary carpet, can make a room,
bringing warm and very subtle colours into the most
austere, poverty-stricken interior, providing accent
where it is needed.

The most likely rugs to turn up in this manner,
judging by some recent sales, are long Hamadan
runners, Afghan, Bokhara, Sarouk, Shiraz, Shirvan.
But it is a tricky market, subject to clever dyeing and
not easily detected repairs.

FURNITURE
MOUNTS

Drawer handles, or drawer knobs, are the most
common of all casualties; whether they are of metal
or wood they seem to be equally vulnerable. The
purist, if he is dealing with an old piece of real
quality, will take pains to replace damaged portions
with as near as possible exact replicas of the original.
Farther down in the social scale he will perhaps allow
himself more latitude, by which I mean that he may
have acquired a modest chest of drawers or a writing
table which is marred by singularly horrible metal
handles, devised by heaven knows what ham-fisted
earnest Victorian who had spent too long at the
Great Exhibition of 1851 and, unlike young William
Morris, had not been repelled by what he saw. The
chest or the table may well be simple and straight-
forward enough as far as the woodwork is concerned,

and its proportions may be good, but its handles offend the eye. They may offend in two ways – if of metal, by their clumsiness; if of wood, by their honesty. This last is a hard saying, but the fact remains that, for economy reasons, much popular furniture of the 19th century was provided with turned wooden handles, as indeed was much popular furniture of an earlier generation. The practice persists, and very agreeable it can be in the hands of the designers of today. It is, however, difficult to make out a case for the defence when one stands before the average Victorian chest of drawers produced for a mass market, and notes the large round wooden handles which screw so clumsily into the centre of the drawers. Better with such pieces – and they are useful enough though not distinguished – to look about for suitable metal handles. It is remarkable how a little care taken over small details of this sort can improve the appearance of a very ordinary piece. Patterns exist by the hundred, and few of us know where to look for them; nor did I until I consulted the antique trade, when I was informed that most people in London went to Beardmore's in Cleveland Street, by the Middlesex Hospital. No doubt some day someone will descend upon Beardmores – some high-falutin' efficiency expert – and redesign the whole place. As it is, it remains a long, narrow shop lined with hundreds upon hundreds of wooden drawers (but for electric light, straight out of Thackeray or Trollope) and inhabited by dedicated men in long, dark-grey coats, who appear to be able to lay their fingers upon any and every possible iron-

59

monger's gadget within two minutes, without the aid of card indexes or similar helps. They move slowly amid the queue of customers – there is invariably a queue – they bite sandwiches between writing receipts, telephones ring, little men in overalls talk technicalities in low voices, an ancient, almost a Dickensian cash register, perched upon a high desk, croaks a raucous addition, and so, sped on our way, with patient courtesy, the kindly, half-amused good manners of the efficient professional for the obviously half-baked amateur, we emerge clutching the particular pattern handle of our ambition, chosen from among a hundred others. Pretty well everything can be supplied in lacquered gilt, silver, bronze, or what is known horribly as antique brass finish, from door finger-plates to the small escutcheons for keyholes, the little pierced galleries for the tops of boudoir writing tables, and such meticulous details as key bows. If the chest is of any quality at all – or for that matter, if it has no quality whatever – it might just as well be fitted with a well-bred key bow as with the normal object of commerce. All one needs is a little discretion; do not overdress a plain deal with a ring handle fit only for an 18th-century ormolu-mounted boudoir writing table in kingwood. The plain man does not wear a morning coat with brown shoes and flannel trousers, nor his handsome wife an Ascot hat with a tweed skirt and cardigan.

WE NEVER HAD IT SO COSY The late-Victorian sitting-room of Plate 28 and the two pages from the Oetzman catalogue of 1896 (Plates 29 and 30) seem to require a few words of comment. The first impression of the room is one of glorious, higgledy-piggledy fuss; in due course, the eye can pick out some details, first of all the squat Eaton Hall chair on its short turned legs on the right. This one appears to be covered not with leather but with a patterned material; the construction is generally sound enough, and the thing can be made presentable with new material and, if necessary, comfortable with the invaluable latex. The sofa will respond to similar treatment. The tripod in the corner by the door appears to be supporting a flower-stand – a degenerate descendant of the 18th-century torchère. The little table in the right foreground comes from India – teak or ebony? – the centre one, on four turned legs, apparently of light covered wood, is so overwhelmed by the cloth over it that it is impossible to distinguish details. The mantelpiece is a clutter of ornament but is not adorned with a cloth with dangling tassels, a much-favoured trimming for this kind of room. Flimsy painted fire screen, good steel fender and fire irons, good Persian rug, lusciously flowered wallpaper. I would guess the 1890's – perhaps a decade earlier. We never had it so cosy.

It has to be remembered as one looks at the pages from the Oetzman catalogue that in the 1890's, before the undoubted blessings of the Welfare State and the less obvious glories of half a century of inflation were revealed to us, £250 was a very substantial sum; as substantial as the chairs, sofa, sideboard and table of this sitting-room-cum-dining-room, the upholstery of which could very well have been in a hideous blend of arsenic green and red. Such objects have survived in quantity and, though alarming at first sight, can be redressed at remarkably little cost. If the chairs' springs have gone, that invariably means a major but worthwhile operation using latex – a godsend to home-groomers. Otherwise, removing the strange tufts from odd corners, chintz works wonders. Tastes differ, but few of us can support both the overmantel and the mirror above the sideboard; this last can easily be removed and, of course, the overmantel as well, but both it, and the sideboard, can be rendered not merely less painful but positively agreeable by careful painting in keeping with modern wall covering and the general scheme of decoration.

The hanging lamp is rapidly becoming a collector's piece. I have not yet come across a Cosy Corner (Plate 30) nor the other strange objects near it.

Chapter 5

There is something inexpressibly sweet in the thought
that, at the cost of a brief bus ride, it may be possible
to buy for £2 something you would have to pay £4
for in Bond Street. The odd thing is that sometimes,
if only very rarely, this can happen; some small
objects, a few Victorian fruit knives and forks with
mother-of-pearl handles for example, which gleam
from amid the surrounding dingy horrors with such
quiet good manners that one wonders what strange
family disaster ever brought them down to the gutter.
Fashion, reinforced by hope, which, as everyone
knows, springs eternal, and by the ever-spreading,
ever luscious grape-vine, attracts thousands in the
course of a year to the Portobello Road on Saturdays
and to what is proudly labelled The New Caledonian
Market in Bermondsey on Fridays. Each is lively
enough, but they differ considerably not so much in
quality as in character. The Saturday Portobello
Road Market provides the visitor with a long series
of stalls on each side of its snake-like length and,
backing them, numerous shops, many of which are
divided up into several compartments jammed close

together where can be found every imaginable small object from watches that may go to Greek vases that never saw the bright waters of the Aegean. A few of the shops deal in furniture of no antiquity, and less quality; none the less, not a bad place to visit occasionally if the quest is for very ordinary, practical pieces which can be groomed or painted or polished into a spick-and-span respectability. One can buy odds and ends of china, remarkably doubtful Old Masters, sinister fetishes from Darkest Africa (I have heard of one or two exceptional rarities of this sort finding their way down this street), mid 19th century jewellery, gimcrack silver-plated goods, mostly Edwardian, so light and thin as almost to dent at the touch. At the New Caledonian Market in Bermondsey – the name is inherited from the old departed Caledonian Market in the Islington area – there is no long narrow street but a wide, rectangular space occupied by several dozen stalls. No shops, scarcely any furniture, paintings only by chance, but a multitude of bric-à-brac and copper pots and pans. Each place has in common a great store of clumsy decanters without stoppers, flotsam and jetsam from a thousand mantelpieces, including those coloured glass vessels painted with roses and other flowers upon a bright blue ground which are well known to induce either ecstasy or nausea in whosoever looks at them. But however disdainful of such things one may be in the rational part of one's make-up, the heart – or is it mere greed? – drives us on; the thought that here is a bazaar – and we envisage Damascus or Samarkand – and that we are, in our small way, Caliphs of

Baghdad, travelling, of course, incognito, rubbing shoulders with the populace, pitting our wits against these shrewd merchants, and fondly imagining that they do not see through our elegant pretences. A useful flower vase, once a bright novelty from Italy for the Christmas trade half a century ago, in these surroundings looks twice the cheerful treasure it was when it was displayed with such exquisite taste in a Burlington Arcade window; the circumstance that at some time during the intervening years someone took a small bite out of it merely adds charm; it has been used and loved. Besides, there are the comings and goings, the leisurely dawdlings up and down between the stalls, the slow, deliberate fingerings of paste buckles, of turquoise and gold Victorian jewellery, of the odd Spode dish, of the half-gallon copper measure from a 19th-century pub ('Only a fiver, sir – perfectly genuine! Might 'ave come from the Marquis of Granby at Dorking!')Not a bad lead this, for most strangers to such markets are familiar with *The Pickwick Papers*. Odd, also, to reflect how these measures, half a century and more ago indispensable furnishings to every country inn, were discarded by brewers and their tenants to be seized upon by the best people as the ideal flower holders, broad in the base, narrow in the neck, and gleaming softly in the firelight. Odd, also, to discover one stall devoted to lamps – oil lamps – upright for the centre of a table, a three-branch hanging candelabra, an adjustable reading lamp clamped to an iron pillar. Odd, too, on my last visit, to realise that not a single carriage lamp was to be seen. Can it be that all survivors from the days of the brougham and the dog-cart are now doing duty on the thresholds of spick-and-span converted stables in Kensington and that none are left to be picked up amid other junk from the not-so-distant past? To sum up, these two markets exercise a compelling fascination upon most people, whether native or visitor. The former, by nature sceptical, are well aware that very little of any consequence is likely to be found in them; the tourist discovers a double charm, that of the souvenir, the authentic small object of no great value, which can bring back nostalgic memories when placed on the shelf back home in the Middle West – memories of the bustle, the chatter, the scruffiness, the Cockney-Englishness of the place and its surroundings – and if there's a fine drizzle coming down, so much the better.

A word perhaps about the older, more famous market – Petticoat Lane, so called – on a Sunday morning. Not a place for antiques or near antiques, nor rubbish furniture. Instead a crowded, bustling, cheerful, mile-long series of stalls where are to be seen bird-cages, dresses, caps, shirts, kitchen utensils, cutlery, kitchenware, shrimps, whelks, oranges, and the world's most loquacious salesmen. 'Bless yer, lidy, I could make more money selling pork sausages outside a Synagogue.' 'Don't go up the road, mister, to think it over; this is my short day – I shall be gone by the time you're back.' There is also, among hundreds of other extrovert characters, one who calls himself Danny the Tie King of England.

Since the above was written a narrow passageway in Islington, Camden Place, a cosy extension of the

66

old Islington High Street, has organised itself into a Saturday market by painting its shop fronts, setting up stalls in available corners and getting itself officially launched by His Worship the Mayor. There is a distinct local flavour about this venture and one is put into a good humour *en route* if one chooses a bus with the right sort of conductor: when we had nearly arrived mine suddenly sang out, 'Adam's Brewery,' and the bus stopped at the offices of The Metropolitan Water Board. It is a gay little experiment, with modern paintings hung up down the centre of the passageway, and a sculptor engaged in working on a portrait head in plaster before a doorway. It is possible that as time goes on more antique shops will open in the district.

Some people are, and for the most respectable of DON'T BE reasons: that wood is so beautiful in itself, its grain AFRAID OF can be so interesting as a pattern, and polish and the PAINT affectionate caress of the years can give it so much warmth and depth. All this is true, but it applies to the finest woods only. No one in his senses is going to paint a set of carved mahogany chairs by Chippendale white in order to conform with an interior decorator's scheme for a sitting-room. This, though, believe it or not, was actually done to a set of chairs in a great house in the Midlands when the Queen and the Prince Consort paid a visit in the 1850's. The chairs are still there in their white coats for everyone to marvel at. But furniture made of the cheaper sorts of wood was, in the past, frequently covered with paint as a matter of course, especially towards the end of the 18th century, when a very large middle-class market was beginning to develop. Chairs, mostly of beech, were painted by the thousand; white and gold for grandiose rooms (a fashion which came over from France) and a more sober combination, black and green, for example, for workaday homes. Paint, too, was an obvious cheap substitute for marquetry, and some of the neatest and most agreeable of the satinwood furniture of those years is decorated with elegant little painted swags of flowers. A liking for colour was no new thing. There was a rage for it after the Restoration of Charles II in 1660, inspired by importations of lacquered chests from the Far East, when it became the fashion for amateurs to experiment with what they fondly imagined was Chinese lacquer. This liking for colour reappeared in one form or another every thirty years or so; you find it in those elegant flowers on papiermâché furniture of the 1840's, as lively as ever in the Morris room in the Victoria and Albert Museum filled with what seems to us rather clumsy furniture of the 1860's painted by Burne-Jones. But this last is rather a special case, well outside run-of-the-mill furniture – the experiments of a few pioneers carrying out individual assignments and with no influence upon current fashions. What the picker-up of this and that must decide is whether the damage is worth repair or whether it would be better hidden beneath a decent coat of paint. If the wood is really fine walnut or mahogany or satinwood or any of the rarer woods he will be well advised to try to match the missing portions from some even more decrepit object he has come across in his search for the unattainable – that is for perfection. Otherwise paint is the answer, and no shame is attached thereto. Nor should it be regarded as merely a substitute for something better. I would not presume to suggest how colour should be used. The obvious thing to do is to tackle the job joyously and if you find the result too horrible, as may very easily happen, to try again. Disappointments, however good for the character, may be avoided to some extent by finding out what our predecessors did. This is not to advocate copying them – nothing can be more dull than a conscientious imitation of a dead fashion – but so that one can see for oneself what others thought was comely and perhaps, by avoiding their mistakes, devise something worth living with; expressing one's own personality rather than that of a man who gave up thinking a couple of hundred years ago. I recommend first a visit to Ham House, where, in addition to a delightful garden and a very grand mansion furnished pretty well as it was in the reign of Charles II, there is some painted furniture of that time. For the 18th century the Victoria and Albert Museum contains every type of painted furniture, both French and English, scattered around its enormous galleries, and there is also the room – the Morris room – already mentioned. For bad, amateurish painted furniture of our own century I heartily recommend the few pieces from the Omega Workshop at the Bethnal Green Museum; badly made, badly designed, drearily painted, and well worth preservation as warnings to all of us to mingle knowledge with enthusiasm and good intentions.

Finally, while we are still on the subject, let the amateur – perhaps at this very moment gingerly dipping his brush in a paint-pot and debating how best to rehabilitate some dowdy, down-at-heel wooden chest – pause and gaze upon one of those marvellous chests made to hold the trousseau of a 15th-century Florentine bride; some great sarcophagus (they were in fact all inspired by marble sarcophagi from the Roman past), carved and gilt and with sides and ends painted with some medieval romance. Let him gaze upon this and return to his simpler task in a humble frame of mind, but knowing that others before him, in Europe's springtime, have not been scared of colour.

HOME GROOMING

Gardeners are all well versed in the day-to-day struggle against endless pests which are intent upon bringing their labours to naught. Wood, even when seasoned, polished and treated with affection can develop disease, and it is as well to keep a watchful eye upon whatever pieces of furniture one may possess. The chief enemies are:

1. *Excessive dryness*, which causes shrinking and splitting. This is on the whole an affliction less noticeable with us than across the Atlantic, where central heating is more common and where it is not unusual to keep the whole house night and day up to a temperature which would be considered stifling in these islands. It is sufficient, though, to turn off the heat during the night so that the wood can swell slightly.

2. *Excessive damp* is no less harmful for it swells the wood and destroys the polish.

3. *Wood-boring beetles:* As regards 1 and 2 no one wants to live in rooms which are uncomfortably devoid of moisture, nor in rooms which are damp, so that ordinary precautions such as making sure that unoccupied rooms are aired at frequent intervals and that roofs and gutters are in good trim should be sufficient. Where people sometimes find themselves in trouble is through overhasty treatment of a minor disaster. Hot water is spilt upon a carefully polished surface and someone impatiently rushes off to dry it under heat. Marks are caused by the careless setting down of a hot plate; wipe with cotton wool dipped in linseed oil, remembering not to leave the oil on too long lest the mark becomes darker than the surrounding surface. Surface dirt will generally vanish after the application of soap and water; if not, try paraffin and soapy water or equal parts of water and vinegar. In every case of first-aid treatment finish off with furniture wax and remember that wood responds to this kind of caress; as far as possible, wax the unseen as well as the visible polished parts, for a furniture wax (there are numerous proprietary makes) is not only a polisher but a food. But there is no need to overdo it – about once a fortnight is recommended by the best people.

Wood beetles: If you should spot a suspicious hole in some newly acquired piece do not imagine that when you lie awake at night you can hear the death-watch beetle. This is a creature which haunts ancient church roofs and similar large-scale structures; it has no great liking for normal domesticity. If your furniture does become infected it will probably be by the common or garden furniture beetle (*Anobium punctatum*) which has an interesting life cycle of about two years and no conceivable excuse for existence. First comes the egg, then the larva, which starts to bore at once, eating away continuously; next it rests near the surface, turns into a chrysalis and emerges as an adult flying beetle eager to breed and starts the process all over again. This furniture beetle will attack both soft and hard woods; another – the Lystus – only green timber. The object of any treatment is to poison the wood so that the larva dies at once if it is present and the wood remains inedible for any further invader. There are several good insecticides obtainable, and it is considered advisable to apply them with a brush or spray in late spring or early summer two or three times at weekly or fortnightly intervals. A more tedious but more fully effective method is to use a hypodermic syringe with a coarse needle on each hole. The pests welcome rough surfaces and cracks at the commencement of operations; they do not like wax polish. It does not exclude them by any means, but regular polishing makes them think twice before attacking.

STRIPPING   The word sounds rather drastic as if it involves the use of a blow-lamp. Very often it will be unnecessary as the removal of surface dirt frequently reveals a fine original surface which requires no more attention than devoted nursing with wax polish. However, something rather more violent is essential if one is faced by very dirty, very obstinate paint or varnish. There are several proprietary strippers which are simple to use, and can be applied with a brush and then rubbed off; make sure the surface is perfectly smooth and clean before waxing afresh – use a little meth. and steel wool if necessary. These strippers may be too fierce for very fragile carving, in which case acetone or carbon tetrachloride can be brushed on with a toothbrush, remembering that the former is highly inflammable (as indeed are the strippers) and the latter anaesthetic.

This is not a professional cabinet-makers' *vade* REPAIRS *mecum*. Therefore, the amateur will be well advised to call in the service of a professional if he is faced with a major repair to a more than ordinary piece. What he can do for himself without losing his amateur status or making the damage worse is the small adjustment involving glue. Small sections of veneer are liable to damage and flake off; first-aid repairs frequently involve no more than cleaning the break and replacing the piece. But first remove any remnants of the old glue with hot water, using patience and remembering not to replace until the damaged area has dried slowly and thoroughly. Liquid glue now comes to everyone very conveniently in tubes; apply pressure while the glue is setting, watch it carefully and remove any surplus before it has hardened.

Liquid wood – also provided in a tube – is good enough for very minor repairs, but it is as well to remember that it is not in fact wood; not *alive* as is wood, not reacting to stresses and temperatures in the same way – in short, inert and unsightly.

TO SUM UP   The finest furniture in the world can look dry, malnourished and hangdog if it is allowed to remain uncaressed at unsuitable temperatures (too cold or too hot) or in unsuitable conditions – too dry or, worst of all, too damp. If fine furniture can so easily become bedraggled and decrepit, so that it seems starved, all the more reason to make sure that one's minor pieces, even one's rubbish, should present an appearance of being well groomed; for all wood – even inferior wood – is to some degree alive and shrinks or expands according to age and climate, and responds remarkably quickly to treatment.

Chapter 6

It is notorious that few of us take the trouble to look TIMBER closely at the various woods of which our furniture is made, any more than we will step aside at Kew to read the labels beneath the trees. Yet the study of both trees as they grow and the timber which is obtained from them is fascinating and becomes more and more complicated if one pursues the subject to include all the exotic woods which have been – and still are – used for the finest type of furniture. That is, however, rather outside the scope of this book. A brief list of the less rare timbers which have been used from time to time for domestic furniture and which one might expect to meet in the ordinary course may be of service, if only as a reminder of the considerable variety used by both country carpenter and urban cabinet-maker. The local man will naturally work mainly in local woods; the townsman, with the world of fashion to cater for, will be trying out imported timbers and unusual veneers.

As for the more familiar woods, custom, if not science, recognises about three hundred varieties of oak, about sixty sorts of mahogany (many of which are not true mahogany but resemble it), and as many kinds of walnut; all of them are normally distinguished in the trade by source or port of shipment. Similarly with rosewood, that purplish-brown wood with a close grain – there are many varieties, and the name is given to several other woods because of their rose-like fragrance. Australian rosewood – with a fine disregard of fact – is now often called Australian mahogany because it is so like Honduras mahogany.

Herewith a list of woods one is likely to meet in the course of several week-end wanderings, trimmed down to manageable proportions.

Alder and its relative *Birch:* Mainly used for country-made chairs from the 18th century onwards.

Amboyna: A mottled wood from the East Indies.

Applewood: One can identify this occasionally as inlay in 17th-century furniture.

Ash: In the past mainly used for chair-seats and the lining of drawers. Lends itself very well for bending under steam heat – a 19th-century development.

Beech: Soft wood in use continually since the mid-17th century.

Boxwood: From the 16th century used for inlay in oak and walnut. Later for border lines on satinwood.

Calamander Wood: From East Indies. Ebony family but brown, striped and mottled with black. Used from about 1800.

Camphor: From East Indies. Unmistakable fragrance. Used for boxes and trunks.

Cherry: Used for small pieces of furniture, mirror

frames, chairs, mostly by local craftsmen in country districts.

Chestnut: (1) *Horse Chestnut:* Europe; yellow, pinkish and of no account.

The Indian variety, pinkish-brown, used only for cheap furniture.

(2) *Sweet or Spanish Chestnut:* Like oak, but without silver grain; better for fencing than for furniture. On the whole best to avoid both kinds.

Cypress: Hard, reddish wood – Persia, the Levant and the Mediterranean shores.

Deal: Generic term applied mostly to wood of Scots pine. Used for modern rough, cheap furniture and as the carcass of grander pieces to be covered with veneers.

Ebony: Many varieties from Africa, Tropical America and the Indies. Colour dark-green to black, and called by various fancy names if it is particularly streaky.

Elm: Both Europe and North America. Dull reddish-brown, and at least twenty varieties. Used a great deal in country districts.

Harewood: A purely fancy name for sycamore stained by oxide of iron to a greyish-green – a favourite veneer for inlays at the end of the 18th century. The word is also applied to the lustrous yellow satinwood from San Domingo which, when seasoned, fades to silver grey.

Holly: Used for inlays, etc. – and sometimes dyed as a substitute for ebony.

Kingwood: From Tropical America; a species of rosewood. An 18th-century importation to France.

The name is said to have been given to it as a compliment to King Louis XV. A rich, dark brown.

Laburnum: Brown to dark-green – Europe and North America. First found towards end of 17th century as veneer. The Indian variety yellowish-red to reddish-brown, seasoning to dark purple-brown.

Lime: Soft, not liable to split, easily carved. Yellowish-white.

Mahogany: For rather more than two hundred years the most admired of woods. Today imports are mostly from West Africa. In the past two sources were important. First, Spanish – i.e. from the West Indies. Sir Walter Raleigh used this magnificent wood to repair his ships, but its quality was not appreciated until about 1715, when small quantities came in. Later in the 18th century, Honduras became the main source of supply.

Maple: Chiefly Europe and North America. Many varieties, the best known probably 'bird's-eye' maple. Used for veneers in the 17th century and 18th, and in 19th for small articles such as picture frames, etc.

Oak: The inevitable wood for furniture until walnut became fashionable after the Restoration of Charles II in 1660; used in country districts for another century and more, and in favour again among architect-designers of furniture from about 1860.

Padouk: Also known as Andaman redwood, Burmese rosewood and East Indies mahogany. Deep-crimson seasoning to a near-purple.

Partridge Wood: Used for inlay. Central America.

The grain resembles the bird's feather. Colour brown and red.

Pine: Used for carcasses and for panelling from 17th century. Later for cheap commercial furniture. A less polite name is Deal.

Purple Wood: From Brazil, very like rosewood and often passes for it.

Rosewood: From both the East Indies and South America. Known to Europe quite early, used as a veneer in the 18th century and popular from about 1800 onwards; so popular in fact that it has come to be regarded as an instance of Victorian vulgarity – a reputation it does not deserve.

Satinwood: From both East and West Indies. Came into fashion about 1770; went out at the turn of the century; back again about 1825 and intermittently in favour ever since.

Sycamore: To many just a forest weed, but it was in the past of considerable service for marquetry in walnut and now for modern furniture.

Teak: Mainly from Burma. Hardly known until the mid-18th century. A beautiful wood, hard and brownish, much in favour during the past half-century for garden seats and for tables and chairs. Always worth scrutiny.

Thuya: An African wood used for veneer from the 18th century onwards – a nice warm brown with small 'bird's eyes.'

Tulipwood: An 18th-century importation from Brazil. Lightish reddish-brown. Used as veneer.

Walnut: Shares with oak and mahogany the affection of most of us. Two main varieties:

(1) *Juglans Regia:* so-called English walnut.

(2) *Juglans Nigra:* a darker sort.

But the amateur will not worry, and moreover will find it very difficult to distinguish between the two. It is said that the cold of the terrible winter of 1709 destroyed enormous numbers of walnut trees in Central Europe; this may partly explain the gradual increase in the importation of mahogany from Cuba and Honduras.

Willow: Hardly a furniture wood, though it used to be dyed to imitate ebony.

Yew: Frequently used for the knobs of drawers and for parts of country-made chairs.

ONE MAN'S SUMMING UP IN 1849

Perhaps at this point a brief quotation from the *Journal of Design* (1849): 'Hints for the Decoration of Dwellings' will serve as well as anything else to describe the confusion of current taste as it was seen by a thoughtful contemporary.

'There is no general agreement in principles of taste. Everyone elects his own style of art. Some few take refuge in a liking for "pure Greek" ' – I suppose by that is meant the neo-classic style of the late 18th century – 'and are rigidly "classical," others find safety in the "antique" ' – by that I think the writer means imitation of what was thought to be Elizabethan – 'others believe only in "Pugin" ' (the earnest Gothicising architect of the day) 'others lean upon imitations of modern Germans and some extol the Renaissance. We all agree only in being imitators.' Have we altered very much in the course of 20 years?

Beds for the Poor. Beech-tree leaves are recommended for filling the beds of poor persons. They should be gathered on a dry day in the autumn and perfectly dried. It is said that the smell is pleasant and that they will not harbour vermin. They are also very springy.

FROM 'ENQUIRE WITHIN UPON EVERYTHING'*

A Good Polish for Furniture which has less the appearance of a hard varnish, and may always be applied so as to restore the pristine beauty of the furniture by a little manual labour. Heat a gallon of water, in which dissolve one pound and a half of potash; and a pound of virgin wax, boiling the whole for half an hour, then suffer it to cool, when the wax will float on the surface. Put the wax into a mortar and triturate it with a marble pestle, adding soft water to it until it forms a soft paste which, laid neatly on furniture, or even on paintings, and carefully rubbed when dry with a woollen rag, gives a polish of great brilliancy, without the harshness of the drier varnishes.

To Clean Cane-bottom Chairs. Turn the chair bottom upwards, and with hot water and a sponge wash the cane-work well, so that it may become completely soaked. Should it be very dirty you must use soap. Let it dry in the open air, or in a place where there is a thorough draught, and it will become as tight and firm as when new, provided none of the strips are broken.

Hints on Furnishing a House. It is only by experience that you can tell what will be the wants of your family, so at first buy merely enough to get along

* 98th edition 1901

with, and add other things by degrees. If you spend all your money, you will find you have purchased many things you do not actually want, and have no means left to get many things you do want. If you have enough, and more than enough, to get everything suitable to your situation, do not think you must spend all you may be able to lay out in furniture, merely because you happen to have it. Begin humbly. As riches increase, it is easy and pleasant to increase in comfort; but it is always painful and inconvenient to decrease. Neatness, tastefulness and good sense may be shown in the management of a small household, and the arrangement of a little furniture, as well as upon a larger scale. The consideration which many purchase by living beyond their income, and, of course, living upon others, is not worth the trouble it costs. It does not, in fact, procure a man valuable friends, or extensive influence.

Index